MW00805439

LIBERTY, EQUALITY, AND LAW
Selected Tanner Lectures on Moral Philosophy

LIBERTY, EQUALITY, and LAW

Selected Tanner Lectures
on Moral Philosophy

John Rawls, Charles Fried, Amartya Sen,
Thomas C. Schelling
Sterling M. McMurrin, *Editor*

UNIVERSITY OF UTAH PRESS — Salt Lake City
CAMBRIDGE UNIVERSITY PRESS — Cambridge, London, Melbourne, Sydney
1987

Preface and selection, copyright © 1987
by The Tanner Lectures on Human Values, a corporation

These essays are reprinted from Volumes I, III, and IV of *The Tanner
Lectures on Human Values*, as follows: John Rawls, "The Basic Liberties
and Their Priority," Volume III, pp. 1–87, © 1982; Charles Fried, "Is
Liberty Possible?" Volume III, pp. 89–135, © 1982; Amartya Sen,
"Equality of What?" Volume I, pp. 195–220, © 1980; Thomas C.
Schelling, "Ethics, Law, and the Exercise of Self-Command," Volume IV,
pp. 43–79, © 1983.

Printed in the United States of America
All rights reserved
Published in North and South America and the Philippines
by the University of Utah Press, Salt Lake City, Utah 84112, U.S.A.,
and in Great Britain and all other countries by
The Press Syndicate of the University of Cambridge
The Edinburgh Building, Shaftesbury Road,
Cambridge, CB2 2RU, and
296 Beaconsfield Parade, Middle Park, Melbourne 3206, Australia.

LIBRARY OF CONGRESS CATALOGING-IN-PUBLICATION DATA

Liberty, equality, and law.

Contents: The basic liberties and their priority/John Rawls — Is lib-
erty possible?/Charles Fried — Equality of what?/Amartya Sen — [etc.]
  1. Law — Philosophy. 2. Law and ethics. 3. Liberty.
I. Rawls, John, 1921–   . II. McMurrin, Sterling M.
K235.L53   1987   340′.11   86-28300
ISBN 0-87480-271-7 (pbk.)

BRITISH LIBRARY CATALOGING-IN-PUBLICATION DATA

Liberty, equality and law: Selected Tanner lectures on moral philosophy.
  1. Ethics
  I. McMurrin, Sterling M.
170   BJ1012
ISBN 0-521-34974-5

CONTENTS

THE TRUSTEES

RT. HON. LORD ASHBY
Former Chancellor of the Queen's University, Belfast,
former Master of Clare College, Cambridge,
and former Vice-Chancellor of the University of Cambridge

DEREK C. BOK
President of Harvard University

DAVID PIERPONT GARDNER
President of the University of California

H. L. A. HART
University College, Oxford; former Principal of Brasenose College and
former Professor of Jurisprudence at Oxford University .

THE REV. CAROLYN TANNER IRISH
Ann Arbor, Michigan

DONALD KENNEDY
President of Stanford University

STERLING M. MCMURRIN
E. E. Ericksen Distinguished Professor at the University of Utah
and former United States Commissioner of Education

CHASE N. PETERSON
CHAIRMAN
President of the University of Utah

BENNO SCHMIDT
President of Yale University

HAROLD T. SHAPIRO
President of the University of Michigan

OBERT C. TANNER
Professor Emeritus of Philosophy at the University of Utah

O. MEREDITH WILSON
President Emeritus of the Center for Advanced Study
in the Behavioral Sciences, President Emeritus of the University of
Minnesota, and President Emeritus of the University of Oregon

PREFACE

In recent years there has been a marked increase of interest in the fundamental issues of both personal and social morality. This growing concern is evident not only in general public discussion but as well in academic circles, where the study of ethical theory and practical morality has extended throughout the curriculum. This is the result, obviously, of the convergence of numerous factors: the technology that has produced the threat of nuclear holocaust and can maintain life beyond the death of the brain, that destroys so much of the natural world and produces deadly waste that cannot be destroyed; the new sensitivity to the injustices suffered by minorities and to the impoverishment and starvation that are the fate of millions; the continuing threat of political tyranny; and the rise of the new religiousness with its impact on morals and public affairs.

Today's moral issues are not new in principle, but they are often generated by social and personal conditions and circumstances that are unique to our world and require, therefore, a continuing process of critical and creative thought. The essays in this volume are expressions of that process on a level of high competence in knowledge, analysis, and humane judgment.

In "The Basic Liberties and Their Priority," John Rawls replies to a decade of criticism of his celebrated treatise *A Theory of Justice*, filling what he feels were two serious gaps in his previous argument. Then, through a discussion of freedom of speech, he illustrates methods by which jurists may apply the philosophical conception of justice.

In "Is Liberty Possible?" Charles Fried advances a liberal theory of law that connects the basic themes of fair shares and private rights in an attempt to resolve both methodological and substantive issues. He then defines and proposes a standard of distribution and treats the problems of legal theory that threaten the coherence of the terms in his proposed theory of private rights.

Amartya Sen of Oxford, in "Equality of What?," rejects the claims of utilitarian, total utility, and Rawlsian equality in the interest of providing a basis for the equality aspect of morality — an aspect that he claims can best be served by the idea of basic capability equality as "a morally relevant dimension taking us beyond utility and primary goods."

In "Ethics, Law, and the Exercise of Self-Command," Thomas C. Schelling sets forth several ethical and social policy issues basic to welfare economics, social choice, and political philosophy. He examines the paradoxes inherent in freedom and contracts issues and indicates paths that should be explored in the effort to ground the sovereignty of the individual on a firm basis.

This is the second volume in a series which includes essays selected from the annually published volumes of *The Tanner Lectures on Human Values*. To date, seven volumes of the Tanner Lectures have been published by the University of Utah Press and Cambridge University Press. The Tanner Lectures, which are endowed by the American scholar and philanthropist Obert C. Tanner, are delivered annually at Clare Hall, Cambridge University, and Brasenose College, Oxford University, in England and at Harvard University, the University of Michigan, Stanford University, and the University of Utah in the United States. Beginning during the academic year 1987–88, the University of California and Yale University will also sponsor Tanner Lectures.

STERLING M. MCMURRIN
University of Utah

The Basic Liberties and Their Priority

JOHN RAWLS

THE TANNER LECTURES ON HUMAN VALUES

Delivered at
The University of Michigan

April 10, 1981

JOHN RAWLS was educated at Princeton University, where he was an undergraduate before World War II and a graduate student afterward. Later he was a Fulbright Fellow at Oxford University. He has taught primarily at Cornell and at Harvard, where he has been for the last twenty-five years. Professor Rawls has been a Guggenheim Fellow and a Fellow of the Center for Advanced Study in the Behavioral Sciences. His published writings include *A Theory of Justice* (1971) and various articles before and since. He gave the Tanner Lectures at Oxford University in May 1978 and the Dewey Lectures at Columbia University in April 1980. He hopes eventually to rework all these lectures into a short book.

This is a much revised and longer version of the Tanner Lecture given at the University of Michigan in April 1981. I am grateful to the Tanner Foundation and the Department of Philosophy at the University of Michigan for the opportunity to give this lecture. I should like to take this occasion to express my gratitude to H. L. A. Hart for writing his critical review (see footnote 1) to which I attempt a partial reply. I have tried to sketch replies to what I believe are the two most fundamental difficulties he raises; and this has led to several important changes in my account of liberty. For many valuable comments and suggestions for how to meet the difficulties Hart raises, I am much indebted to Joshua Rabinowitz.

In making this revision I am indebted to Samuel Scheffler and Anthony Kronman for their comments immediately following the lecture and for later conversations. Scheffler's comments have led me to recast entirely and greatly to enlarge the original version of what are now sections V and VI. Kronman's comments have been particularly helpful in revising section VII. I must also thank Burton Dreben, whose instructive advice and discussion have led to what seem like innumerable changes and revisions.

I remark as a preface that my account of the basic liberties and their priority, when applied to the constitutional doctrine of what I call "a well-ordered society," has a certain similarity to the well-known view of Alexander Meiklejohn (see footnote 11). There are, however, these important differences. First, the kind of primacy Meiklejohn gives to the political liberties and to free speech is here given to the family of basic liberties as a whole; second, the value of self-government, which for Meiklejohn often seems overriding, is counted as but one important value among others; and

[3]

*finally, the philosophical background of the basic liberties is very
different.*

*   *   *

It was pointed out by H. L. A. Hart that the account in my
book *A Theory of Justice* of the basic liberties and their priority
contains, among other failings, two serious gaps. In this lecture I
shall outline, and can do no more than outline, how these gaps can
be filled. The first gap is that the grounds upon which the parties
in the original position adopt the basic liberties and agree to their
priority are not sufficiently explained.[1] This gap is connected with
a second, which is that when the principles of justice are applied
at the constitutional, legislative, and judicial stages, no satisfactory
criterion is given for how the basic liberties are to be further specified and adjusted to one another as social circumstances are made
known.[2] I shall try to fill these two gaps by carrying through the
revisions already introduced in my Dewey Lectures. I shall outline
how the basic liberties and the grounds for their priority can be
founded on the conception of citizens as free and equal persons in
conjunction with an improved account of primary goods.[3] These
revisions bring out that the basic liberties and their priority rest on
a conception of the person that would be recognized as liberal and
not, as Hart thought, on considerations of rational interests alone.[4]
Nevertheless, the structure and content of justice as fairness is still
much the same; except for an important change of phrase in the
first principle of justice, the statement of the two principles of
justice is unchanged and so is the priority of the first principle over
the second.

---

[1] Hart, "Rawls on Liberty and Its Priority," *University of Chicago Law Review*,
vol. 40, no. 3 (Spring 1973), pp. 551–55 (henceforth Hart); reprinted in Norman
Daniels, ed., *Reading Rawls* (New York: Basic Books, 1975), pp. 249–52 (henceforth Daniels).

[2] Hart, pp. 542–50; see Daniels, pp. 239–44.

[3] See "Kantian Constructivism in Moral Theory," *Journal of Philosophy*, vol. 77,
no. 9 (September 1980), especially the first lecture, pp. 519–30.

[4] Hart, p. 555; Daniels, p. 252.

I

Before taking up the two gaps in the account of the basic liberties, a few preliminary matters should be noted. First, the two principles of justice read as follows:

1. Each person has an equal right to a fully adequate scheme of equal basic liberties which is compatible with a similar scheme of liberties for all.

2. Social and economic inequalities are to satisfy two conditions. First, they must be attached to offices and positions open to all under conditions of fair equality of opportunity; and second, they must be to the greatest benefit of the least advantaged members of society.

The change in the first principle of justice mentioned above is that the words "a fully adequate scheme" replace the words "the most extensive total system" which were used in *A Theory of Justice.*[5] This change leads to the insertion of the words "which is" before "compatible." The reasons for this change are explained later and the notion of a fully adequate scheme of basic liberties is discussed in section VIII. For the moment I leave this question aside.

A further preliminary matter is that the equal basic liberties in the first principle of justice are specified by a list as follows: freedom of thought and liberty of conscience; the political liberties and freedom of association, as well as the freedoms specified by the liberty and integrity of the person; and finally, the rights and liberties covered by the rule of law. No priority is assigned to liberty as such, as if the exercise of something called "liberty" has a pre-eminent value and is the main if not the sole end of political and social justice. There is, to be sure, a general presumption against imposing legal and other restrictions on conduct without

---

[5] The phrase "the most extensive" is used in the main statements of the principles of justice on pp. 60, 250, and 302. The phrase "total system" is used in the second and third of these statements.

sufficient reason. But this presumption creates no special priority for any particular liberty. Hart noted, however, that in *A Theory of Justice* I sometimes used arguments and phrases which suggest that the priority of liberty as such is meant; although, as he saw, this is not the correct interpretation.[6] Throughout the history of democratic thought the focus has been on achieving certain specific liberties and constitutional guarantees, as found, for example, in various bills of rights and declarations of the rights of man. The account of the basic liberties follows this tradition.

Some may think that to specify the basic liberties by a list is a makeshift which a philosophical conception of justice should do without. We are accustomed to moral doctrines presented in the form of general definitions and comprehensive first principles. Note, however, that if we can find a list of liberties which, when made part of the two principles of justice, leads the parties in the original position to agree to these principles rather than to the other principles of justice available to them, then what we may call "the initial aim" of justice as fairness is achieved. This aim is to show that the two principles of justice provide a better understanding of the claims of freedom and equality in a democratic society than the first principles associated with the traditional doctrines of utilitarianism, with perfectionism, or with intuitionism. It is these principles, together with the two principles of justice, which are the alternatives available to the parties in the original position when this initial aim is defined.

Now a list of basic liberties can be drawn up in two ways. One way is historical: we survey the constitutions of democratic states and put together a list of liberties normally protected, and we examine the role of these liberties in those constitutions which have worked well. While this kind of information is not available

---

[6] Hart gives a perceptive discussion of whether the first principle of justice means by "liberty" what I have called "liberty as such." This question arises because in the first statement of the principle on p. 60, and elsewhere, I use the phrase "basic liberty," or simply "liberty" when I should have used "basic liberties." With Hart's discussion I agree, on the whole; see pp. 537–41, Daniels, pp. 234–37.

to the parties in the original position, it is available to us — to you and me who are setting up justice as fairness — and therefore this historical knowledge may influence the content of the principles of justice which we allow the parties as alternatives.[7] A second way is to consider which liberties are essential social conditions for the adequate development and full exercise of the two powers of moral personality over a complete life. Doing this connects the basic liberties with the conception of the person used in justice as fairness, and I shall come back to these important matters in sections III–VI.

Let us suppose that we have found a list of basic liberties which achieves the initial aim of justice as fairness. This list we view as a starting point that can be improved by finding a second list such that the parties in the original position would agree to the two principles with the second list rather than the two principles with the initial list. This process can be continued indefinitely, but the discriminating power of philosophical reflection at the level of the original position may soon run out. When this happens we should settle on the last preferred list and then specify that list further at the constitutional, legislative, and judicial stages, when general knowledge of social institutions and of society's circumstances is made known. It suffices that the considerations adduced from the standpoint of the original position determine the general form and content of the basic liberties and explain the adoption of the two principles of justice, which alone among the alternatives incorporate these liberties and assign them priority. Thus, as a matter of method, nothing need be lost by using a step-by-step procedure for arriving at a list of liberties and their further specification.

A final remark concerning the use of a list of liberties. The argument for the priority of liberty, like all arguments from the original position, is always relative to a given enumeration of the

<hr>

[7] See "Kantian Constructivism in Moral Theory," Lect. I, pp. 533–34, Lect. III, pp. 567–68.

alternatives from which the parties are to select. One of these alternatives, the two principles of justice, contains as part of its specification a list of basic liberties and their priority. The source of the alternatives is the historical tradition of moral and political philosophy. We are to regard the original position and the characterization of the deliberations of the parties as a means of selecting principles of justice from alternatives already presented. And this has the important consequence that to establish the priority of liberty it is not necessary to show that the conception of the person, combined with various other aspects of the original position, suffices of itself to derive a satisfactory list of liberties and the principles of justice which assign them priority. Nor is it necessary to show that the two principles of justice (with the priority of liberty included) would be adopted from any enumeration of alternatives however amply it might be supplemented by other principles.[8] I am concerned here with the initial aim of justice as fairness, which, as defined above, is only to show that the principles of justice would be adopted over the other traditional alternatives. If this can be done, we may then proceed to further refinements.

II

After these preliminaries, I begin by noting several features of the basic liberties and their priority. First, the priority of liberty means that the first principle of justice assigns the basic liberties, as given by a list, a special status. They have an absolute weight with respect to reasons of public good and of perfectionist values.[9] For example, the equal political liberties cannot be denied to certain social groups on the grounds that their having these liberties

---

[8] On this point, see *A Theory of Justice* (henceforth *TJ*), p. 581.

[9] The phrases "public good" and "perfectionist values" are used to refer to the notions of goodness in the teleological moral doctrines of utilitarianism and perfectionism, respectively. Thus, these notions are specified independently of a notion of right, for example, in utilitarianism (and in much of welfare economics also) as the satisfaction of the desires, or interests, or preferences of individuals. See further *TJ*, pp. 24–26.

may enable them to block policies needed for economic efficiency and growth. Nor could a discriminatory selective service act be justified (in time of war) on the grounds that it is the least socially disadvantageous way to raise an army. The claims of the basic liberties cannot be overridden by such considerations.

Since the various basic liberties are bound to conflict with one another, the institutional rules which define these liberties must be adjusted so that they fit into a coherent scheme of liberties. The priority of liberty implies in practice that a basic liberty can be limited or denied solely for the sake of one or more other basic liberties, and never, as I have said, for reasons of public good or of perfectionist values. This restriction holds even when those who benefit from the greater efficiency, or together share the greater sum of advantages, are the same persons whose liberties are limited or denied. Since the basic liberties may be limited when they clash with one another, none of these liberties is absolute; nor is it a requirement that, in the finally adjusted scheme, all the basic liberties are to be equally provided for (whatever that might mean). Rather, however these liberties are adjusted to give one coherent scheme, this scheme is secured equally for all citizens.

In understanding the priority of the basic liberties we must distinguish between their restriction and their regulation.[10] The priority of these liberties is not infringed when they are merely regulated, as they must be, in order to be combined into one scheme as well as adapted to certain social conditions necessary for their enduring exercise. So long as what I shall call "the central range of application" of the basic liberties is provided for, the principles of justice are fulfilled. For example, rules of order

---

[10] This distinction is familiar and important in constitutional law. See, for example, Lawrence Tribe, *American Constitutional Law* (Mineola, N. Y.: The Foundation Press, 1978), ch. 12, section 2, where it is applied to freedom of speech as protected by the First Amendment. In *TJ* I failed to make this distinction at crucial points in my account of the basic liberties. I am indebted to Joshua Rabinowitz for clarification on this matter.

are essential for regulating free discussion.[11] Without the general acceptance of reasonable procedures of inquiry and precepts of debate, freedom of speech cannot serve its purpose. Not everyone can speak at once, or use the same public facility at the same time for different ends. Instituting the basic liberties, just as fulfilling various desires, calls for scheduling and social organization. The requisite regulations are not to be mistaken for restrictions on the content of speech, for example, for prohibitions against arguing for certain religious, philosophical, or political doctrines, or against discussing questions of general and particular fact which are relevant in assessing the justice of the basic structure of society. The public use of our reason[12] must be regulated, but the priority of liberty requires this to be done, so far as possible, to preserve intact the central range of application of each basic liberty.

It is wise, I think, to limit the basic liberties to those that are truly essential in the expectation that the liberties which are not basic are satisfactorily allowed for by the general presumption when the discharge of the burden of proof is decided by the other requirements of the two principles of justice. The reason for this limit on the list of basic liberties is the special status of these liberties. Whenever we enlarge the list of basic liberties we risk weakening the protection of the most essential ones and recreating within the scheme of liberties the indeterminate and unguided balancing problems we had hoped to avoid by a suitably circumscribed notion of priority. Therefore, I shall assume throughout, and not always mention, that the basic liberties on the list always have priority, as will often be clear from the arguments for them.

[11] See Alexander Meiklejohn, *Free Speech and Its Relation to Self-Government* (New York: Harper and Row, 1948), ch. 1, section 6, for a well-known discussion of the distinction between rules of order and rules abridging the content of speech.

[12] The phrase "the public use of our reason" is adapted from Kant's essay "What Is Enlightenment?" (1784), where it is introduced in the fifth paragraph; Academy edition of the *Gesammelte Schriften*, vol. 8 (1912), pp. 36–37. Kant contrasts the public use of reason, which is free, to the private use, which may not be free. I do not mean to endorse this view.

The last point about the priority of liberty is that this priority is not required under all conditions. For our purposes here, however, I assume that it is required under what I shall call "reasonably favorable conditions," that is, under social circumstances which, provided the political will exists, permit the effective establishment and the full exercise of these liberties. These conditions are determined by a society's culture, its traditions and acquired skills in running institutions, and its level of economic advance (which need not be especially high), and no doubt by other things as well. I assume as sufficiently evident for our purposes, that in our country today reasonably favorable conditions do obtain, so that for us the priority of the basic liberties is required. Of course, whether the political will exists is a different question entirely. While this will exists by definition in a well-ordered society, in our society part of the political task is to help fashion it.

Following the preceding remarks about the priority of liberty, I summarize several features of the scheme of basic liberties. First: as I have indicated, I assume that each such liberty has what I shall call a "central range of application." The institutional protection of this range of application is a condition of the adequate development and full exercise of the two moral powers of citizens as free and equal persons. I shall elaborate this remark in the next sections. Second, the basic liberties can be made compatible with one another, at least within their central range of application. Put another way, under reasonably favorable conditions, there is a practicable scheme of liberties that can be instituted in which the central range of each liberty is protected. But that such a scheme exists cannot be derived solely from the conception of the person as having the two moral powers, nor solely from the fact that certain liberties, and other primary goods as all-purpose means, are necessary for the development and exercise of these powers. Both of these elements must fit into a workable constitutional arrangement. The historical experience of democratic institutions and reflection on the principles of constitutional design suggest that a practicable scheme of liberties can indeed be found.

I have already remarked that the scheme of basic liberties is not specified in full detail by considerations available in the original position. It is enough that the general form and content of the basic liberties can be outlined and the grounds of their priority understood. The further specification of the liberties is left to the constitutional, legislative, and judicial stages. But in outlining this general form and content we must indicate the special role and central range of application of the basic liberties sufficiently clearly to guide the process of further specification at later stages. For example, among the basic liberties of the person is the right to hold and to have the exclusive use of personal property. The role of this liberty is to allow a sufficient material basis for a sense of personal independence and self-respect, both of which are essential for the development and exercise of the moral powers. Two wider conceptions of the right of property as a basic liberty are to be avoided. One conception extends this right to include certain rights of acquisition and bequest, as well as the right to own means of production and natural resources. On the other conception, the right of property includes the equal right to participate in the control of means of production and natural resources, which are to be socially owned. These wider conceptions are not used because they cannot, I think, be accounted for as necessary for the development and exercise of the moral powers. The merits of these and other conceptions of the right of property are decided at later stages when much more information about a society's circumstances and historical traditions is available.[13]

Finally, it is not supposed that the basic liberties are equally important or prized for the same reasons. Thus one strand of the liberal tradition regards the political liberties as of less intrinsic

---

[13] As an elaboration of this paragraph, see the discussion in *TJ*, pp. 270–74, 280–82, of the question of private property in democracy versus socialism. The two principles of justice by themselves do not settle this question.

value than freedom of thought and liberty of conscience, and the civil liberties generally. What Constant called "the liberties of the moderns" are prized above "the liberties of the ancients." [14] In a large modern society, whatever may have been true in the city–state of classical times, the political liberties are thought to have a lesser place in most persons' conceptions of the good. The role of the political liberties is perhaps largely instrumental in preserving the other liberties.[15] But even if this view is correct, it is no bar to counting certain political liberties among the basic liberties and protecting them by the priority of liberty. For to assign priority to these liberties they need only be important enough as essential institutional means to secure the other basic liberties under the circumstances of a modern state. And if assigning them this priority helps to account for the judgments of priority that we are disposed to affirm after due reflection, then so far so good.

III

I now consider the first gap in the account of liberty. Recall that this gap concerns the grounds upon which the parties in the original position accept the first principle of justice and agree to the priority of its basic liberties as expressed by the ranking of the first principle of justice over the second. To fill this gap I shall introduce a certain conception of the person together with a companion conception of social cooperation.[16] Consider first the conception of the person: there are many different aspects of our nature that can be singled out as particularly significant depending on our aim and point of view. This fact is witnessed by the use of

[14] See Constant's essay, "De la Liberté des Anciens comparée a celle des modernes" (1819).

[15] For an important recent statement of this view, see Isaiah Berlin's "Two Concepts of Liberty" (1958), reprinted in *Four Essays on Liberty* (Oxford: Oxford University Press, 1969); see, for example, pp. 165–66.

[16] In this and the next section I draw upon my "Kantian Constructivism in Moral Theory," footnote 3, to provide the necessary background for the argument to follow.

such expressions as *Homo politicus, Homo oeconomicus,* and *Homo faber.* In justice as fairness the aim is to work out a conception of political and social justice which is congenial to the most deep-seated convictions and traditions of a modern democratic state. The point of doing this is to see whether we can resolve the impasse in our recent political history; namely, that there is no agreement on the way basic social institutions should be arranged if they are to conform to the freedom and equality of citizens as persons. Thus, from the start the conception of the person is regarded as part of a conception of political and social justice. That is, it characterizes how citizens are to think of themselves and of one another in their political and social relationships as specified by the basic structure. This conception is not to be mistaken for an ideal for personal life (for example, an ideal of friendship) or as an ideal for members of some association, much less as a moral ideal such as the Stoic ideal of a wise man.

The connection between the notion of social cooperation and the conception of the person which I shall introduce can be explained as follows. The notion of social cooperation is not simply that of coordinated social activity efficiently organized and guided by publicly recognized rules to achieve some overall end. Social cooperation is always for mutual benefit and this implies that it involves two elements: the first is a shared notion of fair terms of cooperation, which each participant may reasonably be expected to accept, provided that everyone else likewise accepts them. Fair terms of cooperation articulate an idea of reciprocity and mutuality: all who cooperate must benefit, or share in common burdens, in some appropriate fashion judged by a suitable benchmark of comparison. This element in social cooperation I call the Reasonable. The other element corresponds to the Rational: it refers to each participant's rational advantage; what, as individuals, the participants are trying to advance. Whereas the notion of fair terms of cooperation is shared, participants' conceptions of their own rational advantage in general differ. The

unity of social cooperation rests on persons agreeing to its notion
of fair terms.

Now the appropriate notion of fair terms of cooperation
depends on the nature of the cooperative activity itself: on its
background social context, the aims and aspirations of the participants, how they regard themselves and one another as persons,
and so on. What are fair terms for joint-partnerships and for
associations, or for small groups and teams, are not suitable for
social cooperation. For in this case we start by viewing the basic
structure of society as a whole as a form of cooperation. This
structure comprises the main social institutions — the constitution,
the economic regime, the legal order and its specification of property and the like, and how these institutions cohere into one system. What is distinctive about the basic structure is that it provides the framework for a self-sufficient scheme of cooperation for
all the essential purposes of human life, which purposes are served
by the variety of associations and groups within this framework.
Since I suppose the society in question is closed, we are to imagine
that there is no entry or exit except by birth and death: thus persons are born into society taken as a self-sufficient scheme of
cooperation, and we are to conceive of persons as having the
capacity to be normal and fully cooperating members of society
over a complete life. It follows from these stipulations that while
social cooperation can be willing and harmonious, and in this
sense voluntary, it is not voluntary in the sense that our joining or
belonging to associations and groups within society is voluntary.
There is no alternative to social cooperation except unwilling and
resentful compliance, or resistance and civil war.

Our focus, then, is on persons as capable of being normal and
fully cooperating members of society over a complete life. The
capacity for social cooperation is taken as fundamental, since the
basic structure of society is adopted as the first subject of justice.
The fair terms of social cooperation for this case specify the
content of a political and social conception of justice. But if

persons are viewed in this way, we are attributing to them two powers of moral personality. These two powers are the capacity for a sense of right and justice (the capacity to honor fair terms of cooperation and thus to be reasonable), and the capacity for a conception of the good (and thus to be rational). In greater detail, the capacity for a sense of justice is the capacity to understand, to apply and normally to be moved by an effective desire to act from (and not merely in accordance with) the principles of justice as the fair terms of social cooperation. The capacity for a conception of the good is the capacity to form, to revise, and rationally to pursue such a conception, that is, a conception of what we regard for us as a worthwhile human life. A conception of the good normally consists of a determinate scheme of final ends and aims, and of desires that certain persons and associations, as objects of attachments and loyalties, should flourish. Also included in such a conception is a view of our relation to the world — religious, philosophical or moral — by reference to which these ends and attachments are understood.

The next step is to take the two moral powers as the necessary and sufficient condition for being counted a full and equal member of society in questions of political justice. Those who can take part in social cooperation over a complete life, and who are willing to honor the appropriate fair terms of cooperation, are regarded as equal citizens. Here we assume that the moral powers are realized to the requisite minimum degree and paired at any given time with a determinate conception of the good. Given these assumptions, variations and differences in natural gifts and abilities are subordinate: they do not affect persons' status as equal citizens and become relevant only as we aspire to certain offices and positions, or belong to or wish to join certain associations within society. Thus political justice concerns the basic structure as the encompassing institutional framework within which the natural gifts and abilities of individuals are developed and exercised, and the various associations in society exist.

So far I have said nothing about the content of fair terms of cooperation, or what concerns us here, about the basic liberties and their priority. To approach this question, let's sum up by saying: fair terms of social cooperation are terms upon which as equal persons we are willing to cooperate in good faith with all members of society over a complete life. To this let us add: to cooperate on a basis of mutual respect. Adding this clause makes explicit that fair terms of cooperation can be acknowledged by everyone without resentment or humiliation (or for that matter bad conscience) when citizens regard themselves and one another as having to the requisite degree the two moral powers which constitute the basis of equal citizenship. Against this background the problem of specifying the basic liberties and grounding their priority can be seen as the problem of determining appropriate fair terms of cooperation on the basis of mutual respect. Until the wars of religion in the sixteenth and seventeenth centuries these fair terms were narrowly drawn: social cooperation on the basis of mutual respect was regarded as impossible with those of a different faith; or (in terms I have used) with those who affirm a fundamentally different conception of the good. As a philosophical doctrine, liberalism has its origin in those centuries with the development of the various arguments for religious toleration.[17] In the nineteenth century the liberal doctrine was formulated in its main essentials by Constant, Tocqueville and Mill for the context of the modern democratic state, which they saw to be imminent. A crucial assumption of liberalism is that equal citizens have different and indeed incommensurable and irreconcilable conceptions of the good.[18]

---

[17] For an instructive survey of these arguments, see J. W. Allen, *A History of Political Thought in the Sixteenth Century* (London: Methuen, 1928), pp. 73–103, 231–46, 302–31, 428–30; and also his *English Political Thought, 1603–1660* (London: Methuen, 1938), pp. 199–249. The views in Locke's *Letter on Toleration* (1689) or in Montesquieu's *The Spirit of Laws* (1748) have a long prehistory.

[18] This assumption is central to liberalism as stated by Berlin in "Two Concepts of Liberty"; see *Four Essays*, pp. 167–71, footnote 15. I believe it is implicit in the writers cited but cannot go into the matter here. For a more recent statement, see Ronald Dworkin, "Liberalism," in Stuart Hampshire, ed., *Public and Private Morality* (Cambridge: Cambridge University Press, 1978).

In a modern democratic society the existence of such diverse ways of life is seen as a normal condition which can only be removed by the autocratic use of state power. Thus liberalism accepts the plurality of conceptions of the good as a fact of modern life, provided, of course, these conceptions respect the limits specified by the appropriate principles of justice. It tries to show both that a plurality of conceptions of the good is desirable and how a regime of liberty can accommodate this plurality so as to achieve the many benefits of human diversity.

My aim in this lecture is to sketch the connection between the basic liberties with their priority and the fair terms of social cooperation among equal persons as described above. The point of introducing the conception of the person I have used, and its companion conception of social cooperation, is to try to carry the liberal view one step further: that is, to root its assumptions in two underlying philosophical conceptions and then to indicate how the basic liberties with their priority can be regarded as belonging among the fair terms of social cooperation where the nature of this cooperation answers to the conditions these conceptions impose. The social union is no longer founded on a conception of the good as given by a common religious faith or philosophical doctrine, but on a shared public conception of justice appropriate to the conception of citizens in a democratic state as free and equal persons.

IV

In order to explain how this might be done I shall now summarize very briefly what I have said elsewhere about the role of what I have called "the original position" and the way in which it models the conception of the person.[19] The leading idea is that the original position connects the conception of the person and its

---

[19] On the original position, see *TJ*, the entries in the index; for how this position models the conception of the person, see further "Kantian Constructivism in Moral Theory," footnote 3.

companion conception of social cooperation with certain specific principles of justice. (These principles specify what I have earlier called "fair terms of social cooperation.") The connection between these two philosophical conceptions and specific principles of justice is established by the original position as follows: The parties in this position are described as rationally autonomous representatives of citizens in society. As such representatives, the parties are to do the best they can for those they represent subject to the restrictions of the original position. For example, the parties are symmetrically situated with respect to one another and they are in that sense equal; and what I have called "the veil of ignorance" means that the parties do not know the social position, or the conception of the good (its particular aims and attachments), or the realized abilities and psychological propensities, and much else, of the persons they represent. And, as I have already remarked, the parties must agree to certain principles of justice on a short list of alternatives given by the tradition of moral and political philosophy. The agreement of the parties on certain definite principles establishes a connection between these principles and the conception of the person represented by the original position. In this way the content of fair terms of cooperation for persons so conceived is ascertained.

Two different parts of the original position must be carefully distinguished. These parts correspond to the two powers of moral personality, or to what I have called the capacity to be reasonable and the capacity to be rational. While the original position as a whole represents both moral powers, and therefore represents the full conception of the person, the parties as rationally autonomous representatives of persons in society represent only the Rational: the parties agree to those principles which they believe are best for those they represent as seen from these persons' conception of the good and their capacity to form, revise, and rationally to pursue such a conception, so far as the parties can know these things. The Reasonable, or persons' capacity for a sense of justice, which here is their capacity to honor fair terms of social cooperation, is represented by the various restrictions to which the parties are subject in the original position and by the conditions imposed on their agreement. When the principles of justice which are adopted by the parties are affirmed and acted upon by equal citizens in society, citizens then act with full autonomy. The difference between full autonomy and rational autonomy is this: rational autonomy is acting solely from our capacity to be rational and from the determinate conception of the good we have at any given time. Full autonomy includes not only this capacity to be rational but also the capacity to advance our conception of the good in ways consistent with honoring the fair terms of social cooperation; that is, the principles of justice. In a well-ordered society in which citizens know they can count on each other's sense of justice, we may suppose that a person normally wants to act justly as well as to be recognized by others as someone who can be relied upon as a fully cooperating member of society over a complete life. Fully autonomous persons therefore publicly acknowledge and act upon the fair terms of social cooperation moved by the reasons specified by the shared principles of justice. The parties, however, are only rationally autonomous, since the constraints of the Reasonable are simply imposed from without. Indeed, the rational autonomy of the parties is merely that of artificial agents who inhabit a construction designed to model the full conception of the person as both reasonable and rational. It is equal citizens in a well-ordered society who are fully autonomous because they freely accept the constraints of the Reasonable, and in so doing their political life reflects that conception of the person which takes as fundamental their capacity for social cooperation. It is the full autonomy of active citizens which expresses the political ideal to be realized in the social world.[20]

---

[20] I use the distinction between the two parts of the original position which correspond to the Reasonable and the Rational as a vivid way to state the idea that this position models the *full* conception of the person. I hope that this will prevent several

Thus we can say that the parties in the original position are, as rational representatives, rationally autonomous in two respects. First, in their deliberations they are not required to apply, or to be guided by, any prior or antecedent principles of right and justice. Second, in arriving at an agreement on which principles of justice to adopt from the alternatives available, the parties are to be guided solely by what they think is for the determinate good of the persons they represent, so far as the limits on information allow them to determine this. The agreement in the original position on the two principles of justice must be an agreement founded on rationally autonomous reasons in this sense. Thus, in effect, we are using the rationally autonomous deliberations of the parties to select from given alternatives the fair terms of cooperation between the persons they represent.

Much more would have to be said adequately to explain the preceding summary. But here I must turn to the considerations that move the parties in the original position. Of course, their overall aim is to fulfill their responsibility and to do the best they can to advance the determinate good of the persons they represent. The problem is that given the restrictions of the veil of ignorance, it may seem impossible for the parties to ascertain these persons' good and therefore to make a rational agreement on their behalf. To solve this problem we introduce the notion of primary goods and enumerate a list of various things which fall under this heading. The main idea is that primary goods are singled out by asking which things are generally necessary as social conditions and all-purpose means to enable persons to pursue their determinate conceptions of the good and to develop and exercise their two moral powers. Here we must look to social requirements and the normal

---

misinterpretations of this position, for example, that it is intended to be morally neutral, or that it models only the notion of rationality, and therefore that justice as fairness attempts to select principles of justice purely on the basis of a conception of rational choice as understood in economics or decision theory. For a Kantian view, such an attempt is out of the question and is incompatible with its conception of the person.

circumstances of human life in a democratic society. That the primary goods are necessary conditions for realizing the moral powers and are all-purpose means for a sufficiently wide range of final ends presupposes various general facts about human wants and abilities, their characteristic phases and requirements of nurture, relations of social interdependence, and much else. We need at least a rough account of rational plans of life which shows why they normally have a certain structure and depend upon the primary goods for their formation, revision, and execution. What are to count as primary goods is not decided by asking what general means are essential for achieving the final ends which a comprehensive empirical or historical survey might show that people usually or normally have in common. There may be few if any such ends; and those there are may not serve the purposes of a conception of justice. The characterization of primary goods does not rest on such historical or social facts. While the determination of primary goods invokes a knowledge of the general circumstances and requirements of social life, it does so only in the light of a conception of the person given in advance.

The five kinds of primary goods enumerated in *A Theory of Justice* (accompanied by an indication of why each is used) are the following:

1. The basic liberties (freedom of thought and liberty of conscience, and so on): these liberties are the background institutional conditions necessary for the development and the full and informed exercise of the two moral powers (particularly in what later, in section VIII, I shall call "the two fundamental cases"); these liberties are also indispensable for the protection of a wide range of determinate conceptions of the good (within the limits of justice).

2. Freedom of movement and free choice of occupation against a background of diverse opportunities: these opportunities allow the pursuit of diverse final ends and give

effect to a decision to revise and change them, if we so
desire.

3. Powers and prerogatives of offices and positions of responsibility: these give scope to various self-governing and
social capacities of the self.

4. Income and wealth, understood broadly as all-purpose
means (having an exchange value): income and wealth
are needed to achieve directly or indirectly a wide range of
ends, whatever they happen to be.

5. The social bases of self-respect: these bases are those
aspects of basic institutions normally essential if citizens
are to have a lively sense of their own worth as persons and
to be able to develop and exercise their moral powers and
to advance their aims and ends with self-confidence.[21]

Observe that the two principles of justice assess the basic structure of society according to how its institutions protect and assign
some of these primary goods, for example, the basic liberties, and
regulate the production and distribution of other primary goods,
for example, income and wealth. Thus, in general, what has to
be explained is why the parties use this list of primary goods and
why it is rational for them to adopt the two principles of justice.

In this lecture I cannot discuss this general question. Except
for the basic liberties, I shall assume that the grounds for relying
on primary goods are clear enough for our purposes. My aim in
the following sections is to explain why, given the conception of
the person which characterizes the citizens the parties represent,
the basic liberties are indeed primary goods, and moreover why the
principle which guarantees these liberties is to have priority over
the second principle of justice. Sometimes the reason for this
priority is evident from the explanation of why a liberty is basic,

---

[21] For a fuller account of primary goods, see my "Social Unity and Primary
Goods," in Amartya Sen and Bernard Williams, eds., *Beyond Utilitarianism* (Cambridge: Cambridge University Press, 1982).

as in the case of equal liberty of conscience (discussed in sections V–VI). In other cases the priority derives from the procedural role of certain liberties and their fundamental place in regulating the basic structure as a whole, as in the case of the equal political liberties (discussed in section VIII). Finally, certain basic liberties are indispensable institutional conditions once other basic liberties are guaranteed; thus freedom of thought and freedom of association are necessary to give effect to liberty of conscience and the political liberties. (This connection is sketched in the case of free political speech and the political liberties in sections X–XII.) My discussion is very brief and simply illustrates the kinds of grounds the parties have for counting certain liberties as basic. By considering several different basic liberties, each grounded in a somewhat different way, I hope to explain the place of the basic liberties in justice as fairness and the reasons for their priority.

V

We are now ready to survey the grounds upon which the parties in the original position adopt principles which guarantee the basic liberties and assign them priority. I cannot here present the argument for such principles in a rigorous and convincing manner, but shall merely indicate how it might proceed.

Let us note first that given the conception of the person, there are three kinds of considerations the parties must distinguish when they deliberate concerning the good of the persons they represent. There are considerations relating to the development and the full and informed exercise of the two moral powers, each power giving rise to considerations of a distinct kind; and, finally, considerations relating to a person's determinate conception of the good. In this section I take up the considerations relating to the capacity for a conception of the good and to a person's determinate conception of the good. I begin with the latter. Recall that while the parties know that the persons they represent have determinate conceptions of the good, they do not know the content of these conceptions; that is, they do not know the particular final ends and aims these persons pursue, nor the objects of their attachments and loyalties, nor their view of their relation to the world — religious, philosophical, or moral — by reference to which these ends and loyalties are understood. However, the parties do know the general structure of rational persons' plans of life (given the general facts about human psychology and the workings of social institutions) and hence the main elements in a conception of the good as just enumerated. Knowledge of these matters goes with their understanding and use of primary goods as previously explained.

To fix ideas, I focus on liberty of conscience and survey the grounds the parties have for adopting principles which guarantee this basic liberty as applied to religious, philosophical, and moral views of our relation to the world.[22] Of course, while the parties cannot be sure that the persons they represent affirm such views, I shall assume that these persons normally do so, and in any event the parties must allow for this possibility. I assume also that these religious, philosophical, and moral views are already formed and firmly held, and in this sense given. Now if but one of the alternative principles of justice available to the parties guarantees equal liberty of conscience, this principle is to be adopted. Or at least this holds if the conception of justice to which this principle belongs is a workable conception. For the veil of ignorance implies that the parties do not know whether the beliefs espoused by the persons they represent is a majority or a minority view. They cannot take chances by permitting a lesser liberty of conscience to minority religions, say, on the possibility that those they represent espouse a majority or dominant religion and will therefore have an even greater liberty. For it may also happen that these persons belong to a minority faith and may suffer accordingly. If the parties were to gamble in this way, they would show

[22] In this and the next two paragraphs I state in a somewhat different way the main consideration given for liberty of conscience in *TJ*, section 33.

that they did not take the religious, philosophical, or moral convictions of persons seriously, and, in effect, did not know what a religious, philosophical, or moral conviction was.

Note that, strictly speaking, this first ground for liberty of conscience is not an argument. That is, one simply calls attention to the way in which the veil of ignorance combined with the parties' responsibility to protect some unknown but determinate and affirmed religious, philosophical, or moral view gives the parties the strongest reasons for securing this liberty. Here it is fundamental that affirming such views and the conceptions of the good to which they give rise is recognized as non-negotiable, so to speak. They are understood to be forms of belief and conduct the protection of which we cannot properly abandon or be persuaded to jeopardize for the kinds of considerations covered by the second principle of justice. To be sure, there are religious conversions, and persons change their philosophical and moral views. But presumptively these conversions and changes are not prompted by reasons of power and position, or of wealth and status, but are the result of conviction, reason, and reflection. Even if in practice this presumption is often false, this does not affect the responsibility of the parties to protect the integrity of the conception of the good of those they represent.

It is clear, then, why liberty of conscience is a basic liberty and possesses the priority of such a liberty. Given an understanding of what constitutes a religious, philosophical, or moral view, the kinds of considerations covered by the second principle of justice cannot be adduced to restrict the central range of this liberty. If someone denies that liberty of conscience is a basic liberty and maintains that all human interests are commensurable, and that between any two there always exists some rate of exchange in terms of which it is rational to balance the protection of one against the protection of the other, then we have reached an impasse. One way to continue the discussion is to try to show that the scheme of basic liberties as a family is part of a coherent and workable conception of justice appropriate for the basic structure of a democratic regime and, moreover, a conception that is congruent with its most essential convictions.

Let's now turn to considerations relating to the capacity for a conception of the good. This capacity was earlier defined as a capacity to form, to revise, and rationally to pursue a determinate conception of the good. Here there are two closely related grounds, since this capacity can be viewed in two ways. In the first way, the adequate development and exercise of this capacity, as circumstances require, is regarded as a means to a person's good; and as a means it is not (by definition) part of this person's determinate conception of the good. Persons exercise this power in rationally pursuing their final ends and in articulating their notions of a complete life. At any given moment this power serves the determinate conception of the good then affirmed; but the role of this power in forming other and more rational conceptions of the good and in revising existing ones must not be overlooked. There is no guarantee that all aspects of our present way of life are the most rational for us and not in need of at least minor if not major revision. For these reasons the adequate and full exercise of the capacity for a conception of the good is a means to a person's good. Thus, on the assumption that liberty of conscience, and therefore the liberty to fall into error and to make mistakes, is among the social conditions necessary for the development and exercise of this power, the parties have another ground for adopting principles that guarantee this basic liberty. Here we should observe that freedom of association is required to give effect to liberty of conscience; for unless we are at liberty to associate with other like-minded citizens, the exercise of liberty of conscience is denied. These two basic liberties go in tandem.

The second way of regarding the capacity for a conception of the good leads to a further ground for liberty of conscience. This ground rests on the broad scope and regulative nature of this capacity and the inherent principles that guide its operations (the principles of rational deliberation). These features of this capacity enable us to think of ourselves as affirming our way of life in accordance with the full, deliberate, and reasoned exercise of our intellectual and moral powers. And this rationally affirmed relation between our deliberative reason and our way of life itself becomes part of our determinate conception of the good. This possibility is contained in the conception of the person. Thus, in addition to our beliefs being true, our actions right, and our ends good, we may also strive to appreciate *why* our beliefs are true, our actions right, and our ends good and suitable for us. As Mill would say, we may seek to make our conception of the good "our own"; we are not content to accept it ready-made from our society or social peers.[23] Of course, the conception we affirm need not be peculiar to us, or a conception we have, as it were, fashioned for ourselves; rather, we may affirm a religious, philosophical, or moral tradition in which we have been raised and educated, and which we find, at the age of reason, to be a center of our attachments and loyalties. In this case what we affirm is a tradition that incorporates ideals and virtues which meet the tests of our reason and which answer to our deepest desires and affections. Of course, many persons may not examine their acquired beliefs and ends but take them on faith, or be satisfied that they are matters of custom and tradition. They are not to be criticized for this, for in the liberal view there is no political or social evaluation of conceptions of the good within the limits permitted by justice.

In this way of regarding the capacity for a conception of the good, this capacity is not a means to but is an essential part of a determinate conception of the good. The distinctive place in justice as fairness of this conception is that it enables us to view our final aims and loyalties in a way that realizes to the full extent

[23] See J. S. Mill, *On Liberty*, ch. 3, par. 5, where he says, "To a certain extent it is admitted, that our understanding should be our own; but there is not the same willingness to admit that our desires and impulses should be our own likewise; or that to possess impulses of our own, and of any strength, is anything but a peril and a snare." See the whole of pars. 2–9 on the free development of individuality.

one of the moral powers in terms of which persons are characterized in this political conception of justice. For this conception of the good to be possible we must be allowed, even more plainly than in the case of the preceding ground, to fall into error and to make mistakes within the limits established by the basic liberties. In order to guarantee the possibility of this conception of the good, the parties, as our representatives, adopt principles which protect liberty of conscience.

The preceding three grounds for liberty of conscience are related as follows. In the first, conceptions of the good are regarded as given and firmly rooted; and since there is a plurality of such conceptions, each, as it were, non-negotiable, the parties recognize that behind the veil of ignorance the principles of justice which guarantee equal liberty of conscience are the only principles which they can adopt. In the next two grounds, conceptions of the good are seen as subject to revision in accordance with deliberative reason, which is part of the capacity for a conception of the good. But since the full and informed exercise of this capacity requires the social conditions secured by liberty of conscience, these grounds support the same conclusion as the first.

VI

Finally we come to the considerations relating to the capacity for a sense of justice. Here we must be careful. The parties in the original position are rationally autonomous representatives and as such are moved solely by considerations relating to what furthers the determinate conceptions of the good of the persons they represent, either as a means or as a part of these conceptions. Thus, any grounds that prompt the parties to adopt principles that secure the development and exercise of the capacity for a sense of justice must accord with this restriction. Now we saw in the preceding section that the capacity for a conception of the good can be part of, as well as a means to, someone's determinate conception of the good, and that the parties can invoke reasons based on each of these two cases without violating their rationally autonomous role. The situation is different with the sense of justice: for here the parties cannot invoke reasons founded on regarding the development and exercise of this capacity as part of a person's determinate conception of the good. They are restricted to reasons founded on regarding it solely as a means to a person's good.

To be sure, we assume (as do the parties) that citizens have the capacity for a sense of justice, but this assumption is purely formal. It means only that whatever principles the parties select from the alternatives available, the persons the parties represent will be able to develop, as citizens in society, the corresponding sense of justice to the degree to which the parties' deliberations, informed by common-sense knowledge and the theory of human nature, show to be possible and practicable. This assumption is consistent with the parties' rational autonomy and the stipulation that no antecedent notions or principles of justice are to guide (much less constrain) the parties' reasoning as to which alternative to select. In view of this assumption, the parties know that their agreement is not in vain and that citizens in society will act upon the principles agreed to with an effectiveness and regularity of which human nature is capable when political and social institutions satisfy, and are publicly known to satisfy, these principles. But when the parties count, as a consideration in favor of certain principles of justice, the fact that citizens in society will effectively and regularly act upon them, the parties can do so only because they believe that acting from such principles will serve as effective means to the determinate conceptions of the good of the persons they represent. These persons as citizens are moved by reasons of justice as such, but the parties as rational autonomous representatives are not.

With these precautions stated, I now sketch three grounds, each related to the capacity for a sense of justice, that prompt the parties to adopt principles securing the basic liberties and assigning them priority. The first ground rests on two points: first, on the great advantage to everyone's conception of the good of a just and stable scheme of cooperation; and second, on the thesis that the most stable conception of justice is the one specified by the two principles of justice, and this is the case importantly because of the basic liberties and the priority assigned to them by these principles.

Clearly, the public knowledge that everyone has an effective sense of justice and can be relied upon as a fully cooperating member of society is a great advantage to everyone's conception of the good.[24] This public knowledge, and the shared sense of justice which is its object, is the result of time and cultivation, easier to destroy than to build up. The parties assess the traditional alternatives in accordance with how well they generate a publicly recognized sense of justice when the basic structure is known to satisfy the corresponding principles. In doing this they view the developed capacity for a sense of justice as a means to the good of those they represent. That is, a scheme of just social cooperation advances citizens' determinate conceptions of the good; and a scheme made stable by an effective public sense of justice is a better means to this end than a scheme which requires a severe and costly apparatus of penal sanctions, particularly when this apparatus is dangerous to the basic liberties.

The comparative stability of the traditional principles of justice available to the parties is a complicated matter. I cannot summarize here the many considerations I have examined elsewhere to support the second point, the thesis that the two principles of justice are the most stable. I shall only mention one leading idea: namely, that the most stable conception of justice is one that is clear and perspicuous to our reason, congruent with and unconditionally concerned with our good, and rooted not in abnegation but in affirmation of our person.[25] The conclusion argued for is

---

[24] Here I restate the reasoning for the greater stability of justice as fairness found in *TJ*, section 76.

[25] See *TJ*, pp. 498f.

that the two principles of justice answer better to these conditions than the other alternatives precisely because of the basic liberties taken in conjunction with the fair-value of the political liberties (discussed in the next section) and the difference principle. For example, that the two principles of justice are unconditionally concerned with everyone's good is shown by the equality of the basic liberties and their priority, as well as by the fair-value of the political liberties. Again, these principles are clear and perspicuous to our reason because they are to be public and mutually recognized, and they enjoin the basic liberties directly — on their face, as it were.[26] These liberties do not depend upon conjectural calculations concerning the greatest net balance of social interests (or of social values). In justice as fairness such calculations have no place. Observe that this argument for the first ground conforms to the precautions stated in the opening paragraphs of this section. For the parties in adopting the principles of justice which most effectively secure the development and exercise of the sense of justice are moved not from the desire to realize this moral power for its own sake, but rather view it as the best way to stabilize just social cooperation and thereby to advance the determinate conceptions of the good of the persons they represent.

The second ground, not unrelated to the first, proceeds from the fundamental importance of self-respect.[27] It is argued that self-respect is most effectively encouraged and supported by the two principles of justice, again precisely because of the insistence on the equal basic liberties and the priority assigned them, although self-respect is further strengthened and supported by the fair-value of the political liberties and the difference principle.[28]

[26] In saying that the principles of justice enjoin the basic liberties directly and on their face, I have in mind the various considerations mentioned in *TJ* in connection with what I called "embedding"; see pp. 160f, 261–63, 288–89, and 326–27.

[27] Self-respect is discussed in *TJ*, section 67. For its role in the argument for the two principles of justice, see pp. 178–83. For the equal political liberties as a basis of self-respect, see pp. 234, 544–46.

[28] The fair-value of the political liberties is discussed in *TJ*, pp. 224–28, 233–34, 277–79, and 356. In the discussion of the equal political liberties as a basis of self-

That self-respect is also confirmed by other features of the two principles besides the basic liberties only means that no single feature works alone. But this is to be expected. Provided the basic liberties play an important role in supporting self-respect, the parties have grounds founded on these liberties for adopting the two principles of justice.

Very briefly, the argument is this. Self-respect is rooted in our self-confidence as a fully cooperating member of society capable of pursuing a worthwhile conception of the good over a complete life. Thus self-respect presupposes the development and exercise of both moral powers and therefore an effective sense of justice. The importance of self-respect is that it provides a secure sense of our own value, a firm conviction that our determinate conception of the good is worth carrying out. Without self-respect nothing may seem worth doing, and if some things have value for us, we lack the will to pursue them. Thus, the parties give great weight to how well principles of justice support self-respect, otherwise these principles cannot effectively advance the determinate conceptions of the good of those the parties represent. Given this characterization of self-respect, we argue that self-respect depends upon and is encouraged by certain public features of basic social institutions, how they work together and how people who accept these arrangements are expected to (and normally do) regard and treat one another. These features of basic institutions and publicly expected (and normally honored) ways of conduct are the social bases of self-respect (listed earlier in section IV as the last kind of primary goods).

It is clear from the above characterization of self-respect that these social bases are among the most essential primary goods. Now these bases are importantly determined by the public principles of justice. Since only the two principles of justice guarantee the basic liberties, they are more effective than the other alterna-

respect on pp. 544–46, the fair-value of these liberties is not mentioned. It should have been. See also sections VII and XII below.

tives in encouraging and supporting the self-respect of citizens as equal persons. It is the content of these principles as public principles for the basic structure which has this result. This content has two aspects, each paired with one of the two elements of self-respect. Recall that the first element is our self-confidence as a fully cooperating member of society rooted in the development and exercise of the two moral powers (and so as possessing an effective sense of justice); the second element is our secure sense of our own value rooted in the conviction that we can carry out a worthwhile plan of life. The first element is supported by the basic liberties which guarantee the full and informed exercise of both moral powers. The second element is supported by the public nature of this guarantee and the affirmation of it by citizens generally, all in conjunction with the fair-value of the political liberties and the difference principle. For our sense of our own value, as well as our self-confidence, depends on the respect and mutuality shown us by others. By publicly affirming the basic liberties citizens in a well-ordered society express their mutual respect for one another as reasonable and trustworthy, as well as their recognition of the worth all citizens attach to their way of life. Thus the basic liberties enable the two principles of justice to meet more effectively than the other alternatives the requirements for self-respect. Once again, note that at no point in the parties' reasoning are they concerned with the development and exercise of the sense of justice for its own sake; although, of course, this is not true of fully autonomous citizens in a well-ordered society.

The third and last ground relating to the sense of justice I can only indicate here. It is based on that conception of a well-ordered society I have called "a social union of social unions." [29] The idea is that a democratic society well-ordered by the two principles of justice can be for each citizen a far more comprehensive good than the determinate good of individuals when left to their

---

[29] This notion is discussed in *TJ*, section 79. There I didn't connect it with the basic liberties and their priority as I attempt to do here.

own devices or limited to smaller associations. Participation in this more comprehensive good can greatly enlarge and sustain each person's determinate good. The good of social union is most completely realized when everyone participates in this good, but only some may do so and perhaps only a few.

The idea derives from von Humboldt. He says:

> Every human being . . . can act with only one dominant faculty at a time: or rather, one whole nature disposes us at any given time to some single form of spontaneous activity. It would, therefore, seem to follow that man is inevitably destined to a partial cultivation, since he only enfeebles his energies by directing them to a multiplicity of objects. But man has it in his power to avoid one-sidedness, by attempting to unite distinct and generally separately exercised faculties of his nature, by bringing into spontaneous cooperation, at each period of his life, the dying sparks of one activity, and those which the future will kindle, and endeavoring to increase and diversify the powers with which he works, by harmoniously combining them instead of looking for mere variety of objects for their separate exercise. What is achieved in the case of the individual, by the union of past and future with the present, is produced in society by the mutual cooperation of its different members; for in all stages of his life, each individual can achieve only one of those perfections, which represent the possible features of human character. It is through social union, therefore, based on the internal wants and capabilities of its members, that each is enabled to participate in the rich collective resources of all the others.[30]

To illustrate the idea of social union, consider a group of gifted musicians, all of whom have the same natural talents and who could, therefore, have learned to play equally well every instrument in the orchestra. By long training and practice they have become highly proficient on their adopted instrument, recognizing that human limitations require this; they can never be sufficiently

---

[30] This passage is quoted in *TJ*, pp. 523–24n. It is from *The Limits of State Action*, J. W. Burrow, ed. (Cambridge: Cambridge University Press, 1969), pp. 16–17.

skilled on many instruments, much less play them all at once. Thus, in this special case in which everyone's natural talents are identical, the group achieves, by a coordination of activities among peers, the same totality of capacities latent in each. But even when these natural musical gifts are not equal and differ from person to person, a similar result can be achieved provided these gifts are suitably complementary and properly coordinated. In each case, persons need one another, since it is only in active cooperation with others that any one's talents can be realized, and then in large part by the efforts of all. Only in the activities of social union can the individual be complete.

In this illustration the orchestra is a social union. But there are as many kinds of social unions as there are kinds of human activities which satisfy the requisite conditions. Moreover, the basic structure of society provides a framework within which each of these activities may be carried out. Thus we arrive at the idea of society as a social union of social unions once these diverse kinds of human activities are made suitably complementary and can be properly coordinated. What makes a social union of social unions possible is three aspects of our social nature. The first aspect is the complementarity between various human talents which makes possible the many kinds of human activities and their various forms of organization. The second aspect is that what we might be and do far surpasses what we can do and be in any one life, and therefore we depend on the cooperative endeavors of others, not only for the material means of well-being, but also to bring to fruition what we might have been and done. The third aspect is our capacity for an effective sense of justice which can take as its content principles of justice which include an appropriate notion of reciprocity. When such principles are realized in social institutions and honored by all citizens, and this is publicly recognized, the activities of the many social unions are coordinated and combined into a social union of social unions.

The question is: which principles available to the parties in the original position are the most effective in coordinating and combining the many social unions into one social union? Here there are two desiderata: first, these principles must be recognizably connected with the conception of citizens as free and equal persons, which conception should be implicit in the content of these principles and conveyed on their face, as it were. Second, these principles, as principles for the basic structure of society, must contain a notion of reciprocity appropriate to citizens as free and equal persons engaged in social cooperation over a complete life. If these desiderata are not satisfied, we cannot regard the richness and diversity of society's public culture as the result of everyone's cooperative efforts for mutual good; nor can we appreciate this culture as something to which we can contribute and in which we can participate. For this public culture is always in large part the work of others; and therefore to support these attitudes of regard and appreciation citizens must affirm a notion of reciprocity appropriate to their conception of themselves and be able to recognize their shared public purpose and common allegiance. These attitudes are best secured by the two principles of justice precisely because of the recognized public purpose of giving justice to each citizen as a free and equal person on a basis of mutual respect. This purpose is manifest in the public affirmation of the equal basic liberties in the setting of the two principles of justice. The ties of reciprocity are extended over the whole of society and individual and group accomplishments are no longer seen as so many separate personal or associational goods.

Finally, observe that in this explanation of the good of social union, the parties in the original position need have no specific knowledge of the determinate conception of the good of the persons they represent For whatever these persons' conceptions of the good are, their conceptions will be enlarged and sustained by the more comprehensive good of social union provided that their determinate conceptions lie within a certain wide range and are

compatible with the principles of justice. Thus this third ground
is open to the parties in the original position, since it meets the
restrictions imposed on their reasoning. To advance the determinate good of those they represent, the parties adopt principles
which secure the basic liberties. This is the best way to establish
the comprehensive good of social union and the effective sense of
justice which makes it possible. I note in passing that the notion
of society as a social union of social unions shows how it is possible for a regime of liberty not only to accommodate a plurality
of conceptions of the good but also to coordinate the various
activities made possible by human diversity into a more comprehensive good to which everyone can contribute and in which each
can participate. Observe that this more comprehensive good cannot be specified by a conception of the good alone but also needs
a particular conception of justice, namely, justice as fairness. Thus
this more comprehensive good presupposes this conception of justice and it can be attained provided the already given determinate
conceptions of the good satisfy the general conditions stated above.
On the assumption that it is rational for the parties to suppose
these conditions fulfilled, they can regard this more comprehensive
good as enlarging the good of the persons they represent, whatever the determinate conceptions of the good of these persons
may be.

This completes the survey of the grounds upon which the
parties in the original position adopt the two principles of justice
which guarantee the equal basic liberties and assign them priority
as a family. I have not attempted to cover all the grounds that
might be cited, nor have I tried to assess the relative weights of
those I have discussed. My aim has been to survey the most
important grounds. No doubt the grounds connected with the
capacity for a conception of the good are more familiar, perhaps
because they seem more straightforward and, off-hand, of greater
weight; but I believe that the grounds connected with the capacity
for a sense of justice are also important. Throughout I have had

occasion to emphasize that the parties, in order to advance the determinate conceptions of the good of the persons they represent, are led to adopt principles that encourage the development and allow for the full and informed exercise of the two moral powers. Before discussing how the basic liberties are to be specified and adjusted at later stages (that is, before discussing what I earlier called "the second gap"), I must consider an important feature of the first principle of justice which I have referred to several times, namely, the fair-value of the political liberties. Considering this feature will bring out how the grounds for the basic liberties and their priority depend on the content of the two principles of justice as an interrelated family of requirements.

VII

We can summarize the preceding sections as follows: given first, that the procedure of the original position situates the parties symmetrically and subjects them to constraints that express the Reasonable, and second, that the parties are rationally autonomous representatives whose deliberations express the Rational, each citizen is fairly represented in the procedure by which the principles of justice to regulate the basic structure of society are selected. The parties are to decide between the alternative principles moved by considerations derived solely from the good of the persons they represent. For the reasons we have just surveyed, the parties favor principles which protect a wide range of determinate (but unknown) conceptions of the good and which best secure the political and social conditions necessary for the adequate development and the full and informed exercise of the two moral powers. On the assumption that the basic liberties and their priority secure these conditions (under reasonably favorable circumstances), the two principles of justice, with the first principle prior to the second, are the principles agreed to. This achieves what I earlier called "the initial aim" of justice as fairness. But to this it will rightly be objected that I have not considered the provisions made for the material means required for persons to advance their good. Whether principles for the basic liberties and their priority are acceptable depends upon the complementing of such principles by others that provide a fair-share of these means.

The question at hand is this: How does justice as fairness meet the long-standing problem that the basic liberties may prove to be merely formal, so to speak.[31] Many have argued, particularly radical democrats and socialists, that while it may appear that citizens are effectively equal, the social and economic inequalities likely to arise if the basic structure includes the basic liberties and fair equality of opportunity are too large. Those with greater responsibility and wealth can control the course of legislation to their advantage. To answer this question, let's distinguish between the basic liberties and the worth of these liberties as follows:[32] the basic liberties are specified by institutional rights and duties that entitle citizens to do various things, if they wish, and that forbid others to interfere. The basic liberties are a framework of legally protected paths and opportunities. Of course, ignorance and poverty, and the lack of material means generally, prevent people from exercising their rights and from taking advantage of these openings. But rather than counting these and similar obstacles as restricting a person's liberty, we count them as affecting the worth of liberty, that is, the usefulness to persons of their liberties. Now in justice as fairness, this usefulness is specified in terms of an index of the primary goods regulated by the second principle of justice. It is not specified by a person's level of well-being (or by a utility function) but by these primary goods, claims to which are treated as claims to special needs defined for the purposes of a

[31] I am indebted to Norman Daniels for raising the question I try to resolve in this section. See his "Equal Liberty and Unequal Worth of Liberty," in Daniels, pp. 253–81, footnote 1. I am grateful to Joshua Rabinowitz for extensive comments and discussion.

[32] The rest of this paragraph and the next elaborate the paragraph which begins on p. 204 of *TJ*.

political conception of justice. Some primary goods such as income and wealth are understood as all-purpose material means for citizens to advance their ends within the framework of the equal liberties and fair equality of opportunity.

In justice as fairness, then, the equal basic liberties are the same for each citizen and the question of how to compensate for a lesser liberty does not arise. But the worth, or usefulness, of liberty is not the same for everyone. As the difference principle permits, some citizens have, for example, greater income and wealth and therefore greater means of achieving their ends. When this principle is satisfied, however, this lesser worth of liberty is compensated for in this sense: the all-purpose means available to the least advantaged members of society to achieve their ends would be even less were social and economic inequalities, as measured by the index of primary goods, different from what they are. The basic structure of society is arranged so that it maximizes the primary goods available to the least advantaged to make use of the equal basic liberties enjoyed by everyone. This defines one of the central aims of political and social justice.

This distinction between liberty and the worth of liberty is, of course, merely a definition and settles no substantive question.[33] The idea is to combine the equal basic liberties with a principle for regulating certain primary goods viewed as all-purpose means for advancing our ends. This definition is a first step in combining liberty and equality into one coherent notion. The appropriateness of this combination is decided by whether it yields a workable conception of justice which fits, on due reflection, our considered convictions. But to achieve this fit with our considered convictions, we must take an important further step and treat the equal political liberties in a special way. This is done by including in the first principle of justice the guarantee that the political liberties, and

[33] The paragraph which begins on p. 204 of *TJ* can unfortunately be read so as to give the contrary impression.

only these liberties, are secured by what I have called their "fair-value." [34]

To explain: this guarantee means that the worth of the political liberties to all citizens, whatever their social or economic position, must be approximately equal, or at least sufficiently equal, in the sense that everyone has a fair opportunity to hold public office and to influence the outcome of political decisions. This notion of fair opportunity parallels that of fair equality of opportunity in the second principle of justice. [35] When the parties in the original position adopt the priority of liberty, they understand that the equal political liberties are treated in this special way. When we judge the appropriateness of this combination of liberty and equality into one notion, we must keep in mind the distinctive place of the political liberties in the two principles of justice.

It is beyond the scope of a philosophical doctrine to consider in any detail the kinds of arrangements required to insure the fair-value of the equal political liberties, just as it is beyond its scope to consider the laws and regulations required to ensure competition in a market economy. Nevertheless, we must recognize that the problem of guaranteeing the fair-value of the political liberties is of equal if not greater importance than making sure that markets are workably competitive. For unless the fair-value of these liberties is approximately preserved, just background institutions are unlikely to be either established or maintained. How best to proceed is a complex and difficult matter; and at present the requisite historical experience and theoretical understanding may be lacking, so that we must advance by trial and error. But one guideline for guaranteeing fair-value seems to be to keep political parties independent of large concentrations of private economic and social power in a private-property democracy, and of govern-

---

[34] While the idea of the fair-value of the equal political liberties is an important aspect of the two principles of justice as presented in *TJ*, this idea was not sufficiently developed or explained. It was, therefore, easy to miss its significance. The relevant references are given in footnote 28 above.

[35] For fair equality of opportunity in *TJ*, see pp. 72–74 and section 14.

ment control and bureaucratic power in a liberal socialist regime. In either case, society must bear at least a large part of the cost of organizing and carrying out the political process and must regulate the conduct of elections. The guarantee of fair-value for the political liberties is one way in which justice as fairness tries to meet the objection that the basic liberties are merely formal.

Now this guarantee of the fair-value of the political liberties has several noteworthy features. First, it secures for each citizen a fair and roughly equal access to the use of a public facility designed to serve a definite political purpose, namely, the public facility specified by the constitutional rules and procedures which govern the political process and control the entry to positions of political authority. As we shall discuss later (in section IX), these rules and procedures are to be a fair process, designed to yield just and effective legislation. The point to note is that the valid claims of equal citizens are held within certain standard limits by the notion of a fair and equal access to the political process as a public facility. Second, this public facility has limited space, so to speak. Hence, those with relatively greater means can combine together and exclude those who have less in the absence of the guarantee of fair-value of the political liberties. We cannot be sure that the inequalities permitted by the difference principle will be sufficiently small to prevent this. Certainly, in the absence of the second principle of justice, the outcome is a foregone conclusion; for the limited space of the political process has the consequence that the usefulness of our political liberties is far more subject to our social position and our place in the distribution of income and wealth than the usefulness of our other basic liberties. When we also consider the distinctive role of the political process in determining the laws and policies to regulate the basic structure, it is not implausible that these liberties alone should receive the special guarantee of fair-value. This guarantee is a natural focal point between merely formal liberty on the one side and some kind of wider guarantee for all basic liberties on the other.

The mention of this natural focal point raises the question of why a wider guarantee is not included in the first principle of justice. While there is a problem as to what a wider guarantee of fair-value would mean, the answer to this question is, I believe, that such a guarantee is either irrational or superfluous or socially divisive. Thus, let's first understand it as enjoining the equal distribution of all primary goods and not only the basic liberties. This principle I assume to be rejected as irrational, since it does not permit society to meet certain essential requirements of social organization, and to take advantage of considerations of efficiency, and much else. Second, this wider guarantee can be understood to require that a certain fixed bundle of primary goods is to be secured to each citizen as a way publicly to represent the ideal of establishing the equal worth of everyone's liberties. Whatever the merits of this suggestion, it is superfluous in view of the difference principle. For any fraction of the index of primary goods enjoyed by the least advantaged can already be regarded in this manner. Third and last, this guarantee can be understood as requiring the distribution of primary goods according to the content of certain interests regarded as especially central, for example, the religious interest. Thus, some persons may count among their religious obligations going on pilgrimages to distant places or building magnificent cathedrals or temples. To guarantee the equal worth of religious liberty is now understood to require that such persons receive special provision to enable them to meet these obligations. On this view, then, their religious needs, as it were, are greater for the purposes of political justice, whereas those whose religious beliefs oblige them to make but modest demands on material means do not receive such provision; their religious needs are much less. Plainly, this kind of guarantee is socially divisive, a receipt for religious controversy if not civil strife. Similar consequences result, I believe, whenever the public conception of justice adjusts citizens' claims to social resources so that some receive more than others depending on the determinate final ends and loyalties belonging to their conceptions of the good. Thus, the principle of proportionate satisfaction is likewise socially divisive. This is the principle to distribute the primary goods regulated by the difference principle so that the fraction K (where $0 < K \leq 1$), which measures the degree to which a citizen's conception of the good is realized, is the same for everyone, and ideally maximized. Since I have discussed this principle elsewhere, I shall not do so here.[36] It suffices to say that one main reason for using an index of primary goods in assessing the strength of citizens' claims in questions of political justice is precisely to eliminate the socially divisive and irreconcilable conflicts which such principles would arouse.[37]

Finally, we should be clear why the equal political liberties are treated in a special way as expressed by the guarantee of their fair-value. It is not because political life and the participation by everyone in democratic self-government is regarded as the pre-eminent good for fully autonomous citizens. To the contrary, assigning a central place to political life is but one conception of the good among others. Given the size of a modern state, the exercise of the political liberties is bound to have a lesser place in the conception of the good of most citizens than the exercise of the other basic liberties. The guarantee of fair-value for the political liberties is included in the first principle of justice because it is essential in order to establish just legislation and also to make sure that the fair political process specified by the constitution is open to everyone on a basis of rough equality. The idea is to incorporate into the basic structure of society an effective political procedure which mirrors in that structure the fair representation of persons achieved by the original position. It is the fairness of this procedure, secured by the guarantee of the fair-value of the political liberties, together with the second principle of justice (with the

[36] See "Fairness to Goodness," *Philosophical Review*, vol. 84 (October 1975), pp. 551–53.

[37] See further "Social Unity and Primary Goods," footnote 21, sections IV–V.

difference principle), which provides the answer as to why the basic liberties are not merely formal.

VIII

I now turn to how the second gap may be filled. Recall that this gap arises because once we have a number of liberties which must be further specified and adjusted to one another at later stages, we need a criterion for how this is to be done. We are to establish the best, or at least a fully adequate, scheme of basic liberties, given the circumstances of society. Now, in *A Theory of Justice* one criterion suggested seems to be that the basic liberties are to be specified and adjusted so as to achieve the most extensive scheme of these liberties. This criterion is purely quantitative and does not distinguish some cases as more significant than others; moreover, it does not generally apply and is not consistently followed. As Hart noted, it is only in the simplest and least significant cases that the criterion of greatest extent is both applicable and satisfactory.[38] A second proposed criterion in *A Theory of Justice* is that in the ideal procedure of applying the principles of justice, we are to take up the point of view of the representative equal citizen and to adjust the scheme of liberties in the light of this citizen's rational interests as seen from the point of view of the appropriate later stage. But Hart thought that the content of these interests was not described clearly enough for the knowledge of their content to serve as a criterion.[39] In any case, the two criteria seem to conflict, and the best scheme of liberties is not said to be the most extensive.[40]

[38] See Hart, pp. 542–43; Daniels, pp. 239–40.

[39] Hart, pp. 543–47; Daniels, pp. 240–44.

[40] See *TJ*, p. 250, where I have said in the statement of the priority rule that "a less extensive liberty must strengthen the total system of liberty shared by all." Here the "system of liberty" refers to the "system of equal basic liberties," as found in the statement of the first principle on the same page.

I must clear up this ambiguity concerning the criterion. Now it is tempting to think that the desired criterion should enable us to specify and adjust the basic liberties in the best, or the optimum, way. And this suggests in turn that there is something that the scheme of basic liberties is to maximize. Otherwise, how could the best scheme be identified? But in fact, it is implicit in the preceding account of how the first gap is filled that the scheme of basic liberties is not drawn up so as to maximize anything, and, in particular, not the development and exercise of the moral powers.[41] Rather, these liberties and their priority are to guarantee equally for all citizens the social conditions essential for the adequate development and the full and informed exercise of these powers in what I shall call "the two fundamental cases."

The first of these cases is connected with the capacity for a sense of justice and concerns the application of the principles of justice to the basic structure of society and its social policies. The political liberties and freedom of thought are discussed later under this heading. The second fundamental case is connected with the capacity for a conception of the good and concerns the application of the principles of deliberative reason in guiding our conduct over a complete life. Liberty of conscience and freedom of association come in here. What distinguishes the fundamental cases is the comprehensive scope and basic character of the subject to which the principles of justice and of deliberative reason must be applied. The notion of a fundamental case enables us later to

[41] I take it as obvious that acting from the best reasons, or from the balance of reasons as defined by a moral conception, is not, in general, to maximize anything. Whether something is maximized depends on the nature of the moral conception. Thus, neither the pluralistic intuitionism of W. D. Ross as found in *The Right and the Good* (Oxford: The Clarendon Press, 1930), nor the liberalism of Isaiah Berlin as found in *Four Essays on Liberty*, footnote 15, specifies something to be maximized. Neither for that matter does the economists' utility function specify anything to be maximized, in most cases. A utility function is simply a mathematical representation of households' or economic agents' preferences, assuming these preferences to satisfy certain conditions. From a purely formal point of view, there is nothing to prevent an agent who is a pluralistic intuitionist from having a utility function. (Of course, it is well known that an agent with a lexicographical preference-ordering does not have a utility function.)

define a notion of the significance of a liberty, which helps us to outline how the second gap is to be filled.[42]

The upshot will be that the criterion at later stages is to specify and adjust the basic liberties so as to allow the adequate development and the full and informed exercise of both moral powers in the social circumstances under which the two fundamental cases arise in the well-ordered society in question. Such a scheme of liberties I shall call "a fully adequate scheme." This criterion coheres with that of adjusting the scheme of liberties in accordance with the rational interests of the representative equal citizen, the second criterion mentioned earlier. For it is clear from the grounds on which the parties in the original position adopt the two principles of justice that these interests, as seen from the appropriate stage, are best served by a fully adequate scheme. Thus the second gap is filled by carrying through the way the first gap is filled.

Now there are two reasons why the idea of a maximum does not apply to specifying and adjusting the scheme of basic liberties. First, a coherent notion of what is to be maximized is lacking. We cannot maximize the development and exercise of two moral powers at once. And how could we maximize the development and exercise of either power by itself? Do we maximize, other things equal, the number of deliberate affirmations of a conception of the good? That would be absurd. Moreover, we have no notion of a maximum development of these powers. What we do have is a conception of a well-ordered society with certain general features and certain basic institutions. Given this conception, we form the notion of the development and exercise of these powers which is adequate and full relative to the two fundamental cases.

The other reason why the idea of a maximum does not apply is that the two moral powers do not exhaust the person, for persons also have a determinate conception of the good. Recall that such a conception includes an ordering of certain final ends and

---

[42] For clarification of the notion of a fundamental case I am indebted to Susan Wolf.

interests, attachments and loyalties to persons and associations, as well as a view of the world in the light of which these ends and attachments are understood. If citizens had no determinate conceptions of the good which they sought to realize, the just social institutions of a well-ordered society would have no point. Of course, grounds for developing and exercising the moral powers strongly incline the parties in the original position to adopt the basic liberties and their priority. But the great weight of these grounds from the standpoint of the parties does not imply that the exercise of the moral powers on the part of the citizens in society is either the supreme or the sole form of good. Rather, the role and exercise of these powers (in the appropriate instances) is a condition of good. That is, citizens are to act justly and rationally, as circumstances require. In particular, their just and honorable (and fully autonomous) conduct renders them, as Kant would say, worthy of happiness; it makes their accomplishments wholly admirable and their pleasures completely good.[43] But it would be madness to maximize just and rational actions by maximizing the occasions which require them.

IX

Since the notion of a fully adequate scheme of basic liberties has been introduced, I can outline how the scheme of basic liberties is specified and adjusted at later stages. I begin by arranging the basic liberties so as to show their relation to the two moral powers and to the two fundamental cases in which these powers are exercised. The equal political liberties and freedom of thought are to secure the free and informed application of the principles of justice, by means of the full and effective exercise of citizens' sense of justice, to the basic structure of society. (The political liberties, assured their fair-value and other relevant general prin-

---

[43] It is a central theme of Kant's doctrine that moral philosophy is not the study of how to be happy but of how to be worthy of happiness. This theme is found in all his major works beginning with the *First Critique*; see A806, B834.

ciples, properly circumscribed, may of course supplement the principles of justice.) These basic liberties require some form of representative democratic regime and the requisite protections for the freedom of political speech and press, freedom of assembly, and the like. Liberty of conscience and freedom of association are to secure the full and informed and effective application of citizens' powers of deliberative reason to their forming, revising, and rationally pursuing a conception of the good over a complete life. The remaining (and supporting) basic liberties — the liberty and integrity of the person (violated, for example, by slavery and serfdom, and by the denial of freedom of movement and occupation) and the rights and liberties covered by the rule of law — can be connected to the two fundamental cases by noting that they are necessary if the preceding basic liberties are to be properly guaranteed. Altogether the possession of these basic liberties specifies the common and guaranteed status of equal citizens in a well-ordered democratic society.[44]

Given this arrangement of the basic liberties, the notion of the *significance* of a particular liberty, which we need to fill the second gap, can be explained in this way: a liberty is more or less significant depending on whether it is more or less essentially involved in, or is a more or less necessary institutional means to protect, the full and informed and effective exercise of the moral powers in one (or both) of the two fundamental cases. Thus, the weight of particular claims to freedom of speech, press, and dis-

---

[44] The arrangement in this paragraph is designed to emphasize the role of the two fundamental cases and to connect these cases with the two moral powers. Thus this arrangement belongs to a particular conception of justice. Other arrangements may be equally useful for other purposes. Vincent Blasi, in his instructive essay "The Checking Value in First Amendment Theory," *Weaver Constitutional Law Series*, no. 3 (American Bar Foundation, 1977), classifies First Amendment values under three headings: individual autonomy, diversity, and self-government, in addition to what he calls "the checking value." This value focuses on the liberties protected by the First Amendment as a way of controlling the misconduct of government. I believe the arrangement in the text covers these distinctions. The discussion in section VII and below in sections X-XII indicates my agreement with Blasi on the importance of the checking value.

cussion are to be judged by this criterion. Some kinds of speech are not specially protected and others may even be offenses, for example, libel and defamation of individuals, so-called "fighting words" (in certain circumstances), and even political speech when it becomes incitement to the imminent and lawless use of force. Of course, why these kinds of speech are offenses may require careful reflection, and will generally differ in each case. Libel and defamation of private persons (as opposed to political figures) has no significance at all for the public use of reason to judge and regulate the basic structure, and it is in addition a private wrong; while incitements to the imminent and lawless use of force, whatever the significance of the speakers' overall political views, are too disruptive of the democratic process to be permitted by the rules of order of political debate. A well-designed constitution tries to constrain the political leadership to govern with sufficient justice and good sense so that among a reasonable people such incitements to violence will seldom occur and never be serious. So long as the advocacy of revolutionary and even seditious doctrines is fully protected, as it should be, there is no restriction on the content of political speech, but only regulations as to time and place, and the means used to express it.

It is important to keep in mind that in filling the second gap the first principle of justice is to be applied at the stage of the constitutional convention. This means that the political liberties and freedom of thought enter essentially into the specification of a just political procedure. Delegates to such a convention (still regarded as representatives of citizens as free and equal persons but now assigned a different task) are to adopt, from among the just constitutions that are both just and workable the one that seems most likely to lead to just and effective legislation. (Which constitutions and legislation are just is settled by the principles of justice already agreed to in the original position.) This adoption of a constitution is guided by the general knowledge of how political and social institutions work, together with the general facts about existing social circumstances. In the first instance, then, the constitution is seen as a just political procedure which incorporates the equal political liberties and seeks to assure their fair-value so that the processes of political decision are open to all on a roughly equal basis. The constitution must also guarantee freedom of thought if the exercise of these liberties is to be free and informed. The emphasis is first on the constitution as specifying a just and workable political procedure so far without any explicit constitutional restrictions on what the legislative outcome may be. Although delegates have a notion of just and effective legislation, the second principle of justice, which is part of the content of this notion, is not incorporated into the constitution itself. Indeed, the history of successful constitutions suggests that principles to regulate economic and social inequalities, and other distributive principles, are generally not suitable as constitutional restrictions. Rather, just legislation seems to be best achieved by assuring fairness in representation and by other constitutional devices.

The initial emphasis, then, is on the constitution as specifying a just and workable political procedure without any constitutional restrictions on legislative outcomes. But this initial emphasis is not, of course, final. The basic liberties associated with the capacity for a conception of the good must also be respected and this requires additional constitutional restrictions against infringing equal liberty of conscience and freedom of association (as well as the remaining and supporting basic liberties). Of course, these restrictions are simply the result of applying the first principle of justice at the stage of the constitutional convention. But if we return to the idea of starting from the conception of persons as capable of being normal and fully cooperating members of society and of respecting its fair-terms of cooperation over a complete life, then these restrictions can be viewed in another light. If the equal basic liberties of some are restricted or denied, social cooperation on the basis of mutual respect is impossible. For we saw that fair-terms of social cooperation are terms upon which as equal persons we are willing to cooperate with all members of society over a complete life. When fair-terms are not honored, those mistreated will feel resentment or humiliation, and those who benefit must either recognize their fault and be troubled by it, or else regard those mistreated as deserving their loss. On both sides, the conditions of mutual respect are undermined. Thus, the basic liberties of liberty of conscience and freedom of association are properly protected by explicit constitutional restrictions. These restrictions publicly express on the constitution's face, as it were, the conception of social cooperation held by equal citizens in a well-ordered society.

So much for a bare outline of how the second gap is filled, at least at the constitutional stage. In the next section I shall briefly discuss freedom of speech in order to illustrate how this gap is filled in the case of a particular basic liberty. But before doing this it should be noted that all legal rights and liberties other than the basic liberties as protected by the various constitutional provisions (including the guarantee of the fair-value of the political liberties) are to be specified at the legislative stage in the light of the two principles of justice and other relevant principles. This implies, for example, that the question of private property in the means of production or their social ownership and similar questions are not settled at the level of the first principles of justice, but depend upon the traditions and social institutions of a country and its particular problems and historical circumstances.[45] Moreover, even if by some convincing philosophical argument — at least convincing to us and a few like-minded others — we could trace the right of private or social ownership back to first principles or to basic rights, there is a good reason for working out a conception of justice which does not do this. For as we saw earlier, the aim of justice as fairness as a political conception is to resolve the impasse in the democratic tradition as to the way in

---

[45] For references in *TJ* on this point, see footnote 13 above.

which social institutions are to be arranged if they are to conform to the freedom and equality of citizens as moral persons. Philosophical argument alone is most unlikely to convince either side that the other is correct on a question like that of private or social property in the means of production. It seems more fruitful to look for bases of agreement implicit in the public culture of a democratic society and therefore in its underlying conceptions of the person and of social cooperation. Certainly these conceptions are obscure and may possibly be formulated in various ways. That remains to be seen. But I have tried to indicate how these conceptions may be understood and to describe the way in which the notion of the original position can be used to connect them with definite principles of justice found in the tradition of moral philosophy. These principles enable us to account for many if not most of our fundamental constitutional rights and liberties, and they provide a way to decide the remaining questions of justice at the legislative stage. With the two principles of justice on hand, we have a possible common court of appeal for settling the question of property as it arises in the light of current and foreseeable social circumstances.

In sum, then, the constitution specifies a just political procedure and incorporates restrictions which both protect the basic liberties and secure their priority. The rest is left to the legislative stage. Such a constitution conforms to the traditional idea of democratic government while at the same time it allows a place for the institution of judicial review.[46] This conception of the constitution does not found it, in the first instance, on principles of justice, or on basic (or natural) rights. Rather, its foundation is in the conceptions of the person and of social cooperation most likely to be congenial to the public culture of a modern democratic

[46] For a valuable discussion of judicial review in the context of the conception of justice as fairness, see Frank I. Michelman, "In Pursuit of Constitutional Welfare Rights: One View of Rawls' Theory of Justice," *University of Pennsylvania Law Review*, vol. 121, no. 5 (May 1973), pp. 991–1019.

society.[47] I should add that the same idea is used each time in the stages I discuss. That is, at each stage the Reasonable frames and subordinates the Rational; what varies is the task of the rational agents of deliberation and the constraints to which they are subject. Thus the parties in the original position are rationally autonomous representatives constrained by the reasonable conditions incorporated into the original position; and their task is to adopt principles of justice for the basic structure. Whereas delegates to a constitutional convention have far less leeway, since they are to apply the principles of justice adopted in the original position in selecting a constitution. Legislators in a parliamentary body have less leeway still, because any laws they enact must accord both with the constitution and the two principles of justice. As the stages follow one another and as the task changes and becomes less general and more specific, the constraints of the Reasonable become stronger and the veil of ignorance becomes thinner. At each stage, then, the Rational is framed by the Reasonable in a different way. While the constraints of the Reasonable are weakest and the veil of ignorance thickest in the original position, at the judicial stage these constraints are strongest and the veil of ignorance thinnest. The whole sequence is a schema for working out a conception of justice and guiding the application of its principles to the right subject in the right order. This schema is not, of course, a description of any actual political process, and much less of how any constitutional regime may be expected to work. It belongs to a conception of justice, and although it is related to an account of how democracy works, it is not such an account.

X

The preceding outline of how the second gap is filled is extremely abstract. To see in more detail how to proceed, I discuss in this and the next section the freedom of political speech and

[47] See "Kantian Constructivism in Moral Theory," pp. 518–19, footnote 3.

press which falls under the basic liberty of freedom of thought and the first fundamental case. Doing this will illustrate how the basic liberties are further specified and adjusted at later stages, and the way the significance of a particular liberty is given by its role in a fully adequate scheme. (For the notion of significance, see the second paragraph of section IX.)

I begin by noting that the basic liberties not only limit one another but they are also self-limiting.[48] The notion of significance shows why this is so. To explain: the requirement that the basic liberties are to be the same for everyone implies that we can obtain a greater liberty for ourselves only if the same greater liberty is granted to others. For example, while we might want to include in our freedom of (political) speech rights to the unimpeded access to public places and to the free use of social resources to express our political views, these extensions of our liberty, when granted to all, are so unworkable and socially divisive that they would actually greatly reduce the effective scope of freedom of speech. These consequences are recognized by delegates to a constitutional convention who are guided by the rational interest of the representative equal citizen in a fully adequate scheme of basic liberties. Thus, the delegates accept reasonable regulations relating to time and place, and the access to public facilities, always on a footing of equality. For the sake of the most significant liberties, they abandon any special claims to the free use of social resources. This enables them to establish the rules required to secure an effective scope for free political speech in the fundamental case. Much the same reasoning shows why the basic liberty of liberty of conscience is also self-limiting. Here too reasonable regulations would be accepted to secure intact the central range of this liberty, which includes the freedom and integrity of the internal life of religious associations and the liberty of persons

---

[48] Hart argues that a strictly quantitative criterion of how to specify and adjust the basic liberties cannot account for this fact, or so I interpret his argument, pp. 550–51; Daniels, pp. 247–48. I agree that some qualitative criterion is necessary and the notion of significance is to serve this role.

to determine their religious affiliations in social conditions that are free.

Let us now turn to freedom of political speech as a basic liberty, and consider how to specify it into more particular liberties so as to protect its central range. Recall that we are concerned with the fundamental case of the application of the principles of justice (and other general principles as appropriate) to the basic structure of society and its social policies. We think of these principles as applied by free and equal citizens of a democratic regime by the exercise of their sense of justice. The question is: What more particular liberties, or rules of law, are essential to secure the free, full and informed exercise of this moral power.

Here as before I proceed not from a general definition that singles out these liberties but from what the history of constitutional doctrine shows to be some of the fixed points within the central range of the freedom of political speech. Among these fixed points are the following: there is no such thing as the crime of seditious libel; there are no prior restraints on freedom of the press, except for special cases; and the advocacy of revolutionary and subversive doctrines is fully protected. The three fixed points mark out and cover by analogy much of the central range of freedom of political speech. Reflection on these constitutional rules brings out why this is so.

Thus, as Kalven has said, a free society is one in which we cannot defame the government; there is no such offense:

> . . . the absence of seditious libel as a crime is the true pragmatic test of freedom of speech. This I would argue is what free speech is about. Any society in which seditious libel is a crime is, no matter what its other features, not a free society. A society can, for example, either treat obscenity as a crime or not a crime without thereby altering its basic nature as a society. It seems to me it cannot do so with seditious libel. Here the response to this crime defines the society.[49]

[49] See *The Negro and the First Amendment* (Chicago: University of Chicago Press, 1966), p. 16.

Kalven is not saying, I think, that the absence of seditious libel is the whole of freedom of political speech; rather, it is a necessary condition and indeed a condition so necessary that, once securely won, the other essential fixed points are much easier to establish. The history of the use by governments of the crime of seditious libel to suppress criticism and dissent and to maintain their power demonstrates the great significance of this particular liberty to any fully adequate scheme of basic liberties.[50] So long as this crime exists the public press and free discussion cannot play their role in informing the electorate. And, plainly, to allow the crime of seditious libel would undermine the wider possibilities of self-government and the several liberties required for its protection. Thus the great importance of *N. Y. Times* v. *Sullivan* in which the Supreme Court not only rejected the crime of seditious libel but declared the Sedition Act of 1798 unconstitutional now, whether or not it was unconstitutional at the time it was enacted. It has been tried, so to speak, by the court of history and found wanting.[51]

The denial of the crime of seditious libel is closely related to the two other fixed points noted above. If this crime does exist, it can serve as a prior restraint and may easily include subversive advocacy. But the Sedition Act of 1798 caused such resentment that once it lapsed in 1801, the crime of seditious libel was never revived. Within our tradition there has been a consensus that the discussion of general political, religious, and philosophical doctrines can never be censored. Thus the leading problem of the freedom of political speech has focused on the question of subversive advocacy, that is, on advocacy of political doctrines an essential part of which is the necessity of revolution, or the use of unlawful force and the incitement thereto as a means of political

[50] See Blasi, "The Checking Value in First Amendment Theory," footnote 44, pp. 529–44, where he discusses the history of the use of seditious libel to show the importance of the checking value of the liberties secured by the First Amendment.

[51] New York Times v. Sullivan, 376 U.S. 254 (1964) at 276. See Kalven's discussion of this case, ibid., pp. 56–64.

change. A series of Supreme Court cases from *Schenck* to *Branden-burg* has dealt with this problem; it was in *Schenck* that Holmes formulated the well-known "clear and present danger rule," which was effectively emasculated by the way it was understood and applied in *Dennis*. Thus I shall briefly discuss the problem of subversive advocacy to illustrate how the more particular liberties are specified under freedom of political speech.

Let us begin by noting why subversive advocacy becomes the central problem once there is agreement that all general discussion of doctrine as well as of the justice of the basic structure and its policies is fully protected. Kalven rightly emphasizes that it is with such advocacy that the grounds for restricting political speech seem most persuasive, yet at the same time these grounds run counter to the fundamental values of a democratic society.[52] Free political speech is not only required if citizens are to exercise their moral powers in the first fundamental case, but free speech to-gether with the just political procedure specified by the constitu-tion provides an alternative to revolution and the use of force which can be so destructive to the basic liberties. There must be some point at which political speech becomes so closely connected with the use of force that it may be properly restricted. But what is this point?

In *Gitlow* the Supreme Court held that subversive advocacy was not protected by the First Amendment when the legislature had determined that advocating the overthrow of organized gov-ernment by force involves the danger of substantive evils which the state through its police power may prevent. The Court pre-sumed that the legislature's determination of the danger was cor-rect, in the absence of strong grounds to the contrary. *Branden-burg*, which is now controlling and therefore ends the story for

[52] Here and throughout this section and the next I am much indebted to Kalven's discussion of subversive advocacy in the forthcoming book *A Worthy Tradition*. I am most grateful to James Kalven for letting me read the relevant part of the manu-script of this very important work.

the moment, overrules *Gitlow* (implied by its explicit overruling of Whitney). Here the Court adopts the principle that "the constitutional guarantees of free speech and press do not permit a State to forbid or to proscribe advocacy of the use of force or of law violation except where such advocacy is directed to inciting or producing imminent lawless action and is likely to incite or produce such action."[53] Observe that the proscribed kind of speech must be both intentional and directed to producing imminent lawless action as well as delivered in circumstances which make this result likely.

While *Brandenburg* leaves several important questions unanswered, it is much better constitutional doctrine than what preceded it, especially when it is read together with *N. Y. Times* v. *Sullivan* and the later *N.Y. Times* v. *United States*.[54] (These three cases between them cover the three fixed points previously mentioned.) The reason is that *Brandenburg* draws the line to protected speech so as to recognize the legitimacy of subversive advocacy in a constitutional democracy. It is tempting to think of political speech which advocates revolution as similar to incitement to an ordinary crime such as arson or assault, or even to causing a dangerous stampede, as in Holmes's utterly trivial example of someone falsely shouting "Fire!" in a crowded theater. (This example is trivial because it has point only against the view, defended by no one, that all speech of whatever kind is protected, perhaps because it is thought that speech is not action and only action is punishable.[55]) But revolution is a very special crime; while

---

[53] Brandenburg v. Ohio, 395 U.S. 444 (1969) at 447.

[54] New York Times v. United States, 403 U.S. 713. See also Near v. Minnesota, 283 U.S. 697, the major earlier case on prior restraint.

[55] A similar critical view of Holmes's example is found in Kalven's manuscript, footnote 52. Thomas Emerson, in *The System of Freedom of Expression* (New York: Random House, 1970), attempts to give an account of free speech based on a distinction between speech and action, the one protected, the other not. But as T. M. Scanlon points out in his "A Theory of Freedom of Expression," *Philosophy and Public Affairs*, vol. 1, no. 2 (Winter 1972), pp. 207–8, a view of this kind puts the main burden on how this distinction is to be made and is bound to depart widely from the ordinary use

even a constitutional regime must have the legal right to punish violations of its laws, these laws even when enacted by due process may be more or less unjust, or may appear to be so to significant groups in society who find them oppressive. Historically, the question of when resistance and revolution are justified is one of the deepest political questions. Most recently, the problems of civil disobedience and conscientious refusal to military service, occasioned by what was widely regarded as an unjust war, have been profoundly troubling and are still unresolved. Thus, although there is agreement that arson, murder, and lynching are crimes, this is not the case with resistance and revolution whenever they become serious questions even in a moderately well-governed democratic regime (as opposed to a well-ordered society, where by definition the problem does not arise). Or more accurately, they are agreed to be crimes only in the legal sense of being contrary to law, but to a law that in the eyes of many has lost its legitimacy. That subversive advocacy is widespread enough to pose a live political question is a sign of an impending crisis rooted in the perception of significant groups that the basic structure is unjust and oppressive. It is a warning that they are ready to entertain drastic steps because other ways of redressing their grievances have failed.

All this is long familiar. I mention these matters only to recall the obvious: that subversive advocacy is always part of a more comprehensive political view; and in the case of so-called "criminal syndicalism" (the statutory offense in many of the historical cases), the political view was socialism, one of the most comprehensive political doctrines ever formulated. As Kalven observes, revolutionaries don't simply shout: "Revolt! Revolt!" They give reasons.[56] To repress subversive advocacy is to suppress the dis-

---

of the words "speech" and "conduct." For an instructive and sympathetic account of how such a view might be developed, see Alan Fuchs, "Further Steps Toward a General Theory of Freedom of Expression," *William and Mary Law Review*, vol. 18 (Winter 1976).

[56] See Kalven's manuscript, footnote 52.

cussion of these reasons, and to do this is to restrict the free and informed public use of our reason in judging the justice of the basic structure and its social policies. And thus the basic liberty of freedom of thought is violated.

As a further consideration, a conception of justice for a democratic society presupposes a theory of human nature. It does so, first, in regard to whether the ideals expressed by its conceptions of the person and of a well-ordered society are feasible in view of the capacities of human nature and the requirements of social life.[57] And second, and most relevant here, it presupposes a theory of how democratic institutions are likely to work and of how fragile and unstable they are likely to be. The Court said in *Gitlow*:

> That utterances inciting to the overthrow of organized government by unlawful means, present a sufficient danger of substantive evil to bring their punishment within the range of legislative discretion, is clear. Such utterances, by their very nature, involve danger to the public peace and to the security of the State . . . . And the immediate danger is none the less real and substantial, because the effect of a given utterance cannot be accurately foreseen. A single revolutionary spark may kindle a fire that, smouldering for a time, may burst into a sweeping and destructive conflagration.[58]

This passage suggests a view, not unlike that of Hobbes, of the very great fragility and instability of political arrangements. Even in a democratic regime, it supposes that volatile and destructive social forces may be set going by revolutionary speech, to smoulder unrecognized below the surface calm of political life only to break out suddenly with uncontrollable force that sweeps all before it. If free political speech is guaranteed, however, serious grievances do not go unrecognized or suddenly become highly dangerous.

[57] See "Kantian Constructivism in Moral Theory," pp. 534–35, footnote 3.

[58] Gitlow v. New York, 268 U.S. 652 (1925) at 669.

They are publicly voiced; and in a moderately well-governed regime they are at least to some degree taken into account. Moreover, the theory of how democratic institutions work must agree with Locke that persons are capable of a certain natural political virtue and do not engage in resistance and revolution unless their social position in the basic structure is seriously unjust and this condition has persisted over some period of time and seems to be removable by no other means.[59] Thus the basic institutions of a moderately well-governed democratic society are not so fragile or unstable as to be brought down by subversive advocacy alone. Indeed, a wise political leadership in such a society takes this advocacy as a warning that fundamental changes may be necessary; and what changes are required is known in part from the more comprehensive political view used to explain and justify the advocacy of resistance and revolution.

It remains to connect the preceding remarks with the deliberations of delegates in a constitutional convention who represent the rational interest of equal citizens in a fully adequate scheme of basic liberties. We simply say that these remarks explain why the delegates would draw the line between protected and unprotected political speech not (as *Gitlow* does) at subversive advocacy as such but (as *Brandenburg* does) at subversive advocacy when it is both directed to inciting imminent and unlawful use of force and likely to achieve this result. The discussion illustrates how the freedom of political speech as a basic liberty is specified and adjusted at later stages so as to protect its central range, namely the free public use of our reason in all matters that concern the justice of the basic structure and its social policies.

XI

In order to fill out the preceding discussion of free political speech I shall make a few observations about the so-called "clear

---

[59] See Locke's Second Treatise of Government, sections 223–30. For the idea of natural political virtue in Locke, see Peter Laslett's introduction to his critical edition:

and present danger rule." This rule is familiar and has an important place in the history of constitutional doctrine. It may prove instructive to ask why it has fallen into disrepute. I shall assume throughout that the rule is intended to apply to political speech, and in particular to subversive advocacy, to decide when such speech and advocacy may be restricted. I assume also that the rule concerns the content of speech and not merely its regulation, since as a rule for regulating speech, it raises altogether different questions and may often prove acceptable.[60]

Let's begin by considering Holmes's original formulation of the rule in *Schenck*. It runs as follows: "The question in every case is whether the words are used in such circumstances and are of such a nature as to create a clear and present danger that they will bring about the substantive evils that Congress has a right to prevent. It is a question of proximity and degree."[61] This rule has a certain similarity with *Brandenburg*; we have only to suppose that the words "clear and present danger" refer to imminent lawless action. But this similarity is deceptive, as we can see by noting the reasons why Holmes's rule, and even Brandeis's statement of it in *Whitney*, proves unsatisfactory. One reason is that the roots of the rule in Holmes's formulation are in his account of the law of attempts in his book *The Common Law*.[62] The law of attempts tries to bridge the gap between what the defendant did and the completed crime as defined by statute. In attempts, and similarly in the case of free speech, actions with no serious consequences can be ignored. The traditional view of attempts required specific intent to do the particular offense. For Holmes

John Locke, Two Treatises of Government (Cambridge: Cambridge University Press, 1960), pp. 108–11.

[60] My account of the clear and present danger rule has been much influenced by Kalven's manuscript, footnote 52, and by Meiklejohn's *Free Speech and Its Relation to Self-Government*, ch. 2, footnote 11.

[61] Schenck v. United States, 249 U.S. 47 at 52.

[62] For the significance of this origin of the rule, see Yosal Rogat, "Mr. Justice Holmes: The Judge as Spectator," *University of Chicago Law Review*, vol. 31 (Winter 1964), pp. 215–17.

intent was relevant only because it increased the likelihood that what the agent does will cause actual harm. When applied to free speech this view has the virtue of tolerating innocuous speech and does not justify punishment for thoughts alone. But it is an unsatisfactory basis for the constitutional protection of political speech, since it leads us to focus on how dangerous the speech in question is, as if by being somehow dangerous, speech becomes an ordinary crime.

The essential thing, however, is the kind of speech in question and the role of this kind of speech in a democratic regime. And *of course* political speech which expresses doctrines we reject, or find contrary to our interests, all too easily strikes us as dangerous. A just constitution protects and gives priority to certain kinds of speech in virtue of their significance in what I have called "the two fundamental cases." Because Holmes's rule ignores the role and significance of political speech, it is not surprising that he should have written the unanimous opinions upholding the convictions of *Schenck* and *Debs* and dissented in *Abrams* and *Gitlow*. It might appear that he perceived the political speech of the socialists Schenck and Debs as sufficiently dangerous when the country was at war, while he dissented in *Abrams* and *Gitlow* because he perceived the political activities of the defendants as harmless.

This impression is strengthened by the fact that the words which follow the statement of the rule (cited above) are these: "When a nation is at war many things that might be said in time of peace are such a hindrance to its effort that their utterance will not be endured as long as men fight and that no Court could regard them as protected by any constitutional right. It seems to be admitted that if an actual obstruction of the recruiting service were proved, liability for words that produced that effect might be enforced."

If we look at Holmes's opinion in *Debs*, the socialist candidate for the presidency is not accused of encouraging or inciting imminent and lawless violence, and so of creating a clear and present danger in that sense. As reported in the Court's opinion, Debs in a public speech simply attacked the war as having been declared by the master class for its own ends and maintained that the working class had everything to lose, including their lives, and so on. Holmes finds it sufficient to uphold the sentence of ten years' imprisonment that one purpose of the speech "was to oppose not only war in general but this war, and that the opposition was so expressed that its natural and intended effect would be to obstruct recruiting. If that was intended, and if, in all the circumstances, that would be the probable effect, it would not be protected by reason of its being part of a general program and expressions of a general and conscientious belief." [63] Here the natural and intended effect to which Holmes refers is surely that those who heard or read about Debs's speech would be convinced or encouraged by what he said and resolve to conduct themselves accordingly. It must be the consequences of political conviction and resolve which Holmes sees as the clear and present danger. Holmes is little troubled by the constitutional question raised in *Debs*, even though the case involves a leader of a political party, already four times its candidate for the presidency. Holmes devotes little time to it. He is content to say in one sentence, which immediately follows the passage just quoted, that *Schenck* settles the matter. This sentence reads: "The chief defences upon which the defendant seemed willing to rely were the denial that we have dealt with and that based upon the First Amendment to the Constitution, disposed of in Schenck v. United States . . . ." Holmes is here referring to the fact that Debs had maintained that the statute under which he was indicted is unconstitutional as interfering with free speech contrary to the First Amendment.

Brandeis's concurring opinion in *Whitney* is another matter. Along with Hand's opinion in *Masses*, it was one of the memorable steps in the development of doctrine. Early in the opinion

---

[63] Debs v. United States, 249 U.S. 211 at 215.

Brandeis states that the right of free speech, the right to teach, and the right of assembly are "fundamental rights" protected by the First Amendment. These rights, even though fundamental, are not absolute; their exercise is subject to restriction "if the particular restriction proposed is required in order to protect the State from destruction or serious injury, political, economic, or moral." [64] He then proceeds to refer to the *Schenck* formulation of the clear and present danger rule and seeks to fix more exactly the standard by which it is to be applied; that is, to say when a danger is clear, how remote it may be and yet be held present, and what degree of evil is necessary to justify a restriction of free speech.

The strength of Brandeis's opinion lies in its recognition of the role of free political speech in a democratic regime and the connection he establishes between this role and the requirement that the danger must be imminent and not merely likely sometime in the future. The idea is that the evil should be "so imminent that it may befall before there is opportunity for full discussion. If there is time to expose through discussion the falsehoods and fallacies, to avert the evil by the processes of education, the remedy to be applied is more speech, not enforced silence. Only an emergency can justify repression. Such must be the rule if authority is to be reconciled with freedom." [65] Later on he says, referring to advocacy and not incitement: "The fact that speech is likely to result in some violence or in the destruction of property is not enough to justify its suppression. There must be the probability of serious injury to the State. Among free men the deterrents ordinarily applied to prevent crime are education and punishment for violations of the law, not abridgment of the rights of free speech and assembly." [66] And finally, in rejecting the grounds of the majority opinion, Brandeis concludes: "I am unable to

---

[64] 274 U.S. 357 at 373. For Hand's opinion in *Masses*, see Masses Publishing v. Patten, 244 Fed. 535 (S.D.N.Y. 1917).

[65] Ibid., at 377.

[66] Ibid., at 378.

assent to the suggestion in the opinion of the Court that assembling with a political party, formed to advocate the desirability of a proletarian revolution by mass action at some date necessarily far in the future, is not a right within the protection of the Fourteenth Amendment." [67] All of this and much else is plainly an advance in fixing the standard by which the clear and present danger rule is to be applied.

Yet in *Dennis* the Court interprets the rule in such a way as to emasculate it as a standard for protecting free political speech. For here the Court adopts Hand's formulation of the rule which runs as follows: "In each case [courts] must ask whether the gravity of the 'evil' discounted by its improbability, justifies such an invasion of free speech as is necessary to avoid the danger." [68] Expressed this way the rule does not require that the evil be imminent. Even though the evil is remote, it may be enough that it is great and sufficiently probable. The rule now reads like a maxim of decision theory appropriate to a constitutional doctrine that justifies all decisions by what is necessary to maximize the net sum of social advantages, or the net balance of social values. Given this background conception, it can seem simply irrational to require that the danger be in any strict sense imminent. This is because the principle to maximize the net sum of social advantages (or the net balance of social values) does not allow us to give any greater weight to what is imminent than what the improbability and the value of future advantages permit. Free political speech is assessed as a means and as an end in itself along with everything else. Thus Brandeis's idea that the danger must be imminent because free speech is the constitutionally approved way to protect against future danger may appear irrational in many situations and sometimes even suicidal. His account of free speech needs to be further elaborated in order to make it convincing. This is because

[67] Ibid., at 379.

[68] 341 U.S. 494 at 510, citing 183 F. 2d. at 212.

the clear and present danger rule originates from a different view than the constitutional doctrine he is attempting to develop.[69] What is required is to specify more sharply the kind of situation which can justify the restriction of free political speech. Brandeis refers to protecting "the state from destruction," and from "serious injury, political, economic and moral." These phrases are too loose and cover too much ground. Let's see how Brandeis's view might be elaborated to accord with the priority of liberty.

The essential thing is to recognize the difference between what I shall call "a constitutional crisis of the requisite kind" and an emergency in which there is a present or foreseeable threat of serious injury, political, economic, and moral, or even of the destruction of the state. For example, the fact that the country is at war and such an emergency exists does not entail that a constitutional crisis of the requisite kind also exists. The reason is that to restrict or suppress free political speech, including subversive advocacy, always implies at least a partial suspension of democracy. A constitutional doctrine which gives priority to free political speech and other basic liberties must hold that to impose such a suspension requires the existence of a constitutional crisis in which free political institutions cannot effectively operate or take the required measures to preserve themselves. A number of historical cases illustrate that free democratic political institutions have operated effectively to take the necessary measures in serious emergencies without restricting free political speech; and in some cases where such restrictions have been imposed they were unneces-

---

[69] The basis of Brandeis's own view is best expressed, I think, in the well-known paragraph which begins: "Those who won our independence believed that the final end of the State was to make men free to develop their faculties; and that in its government the deliberative forces should prevail over the arbitrary." This paragraph ends: "Believing in the power of reason as applied through public discussion, they eschewed the silence coerced by law — the argument of force in its worst form. Recognizing the occasional tyrannies of governing majorities, they amended the Constitution so that free speech and assembly should be guaranteed." It is no criticism of this fine paragraph to recognize that by itself it does not remedy the defect of Brandeis's formulation of the clear and present danger rule.

sary and made no contribution whatever to meeting the emergency. It is not enough for those in authority to say that a grave danger exists and that they are taking effective steps to prevent it. A well-designed constitution includes democratic procedures for dealing with emergencies. Thus as a matter of constitutional doctrine the priority of liberty implies that free political speech cannot be restricted unless it can be reasonably argued from the specific nature of the present situation that there exists a constitutional crisis in which democratic institutions cannot work effectively and their procedures for dealing with emergencies cannot operate.

In the constitutional doctrine proposed, then, it is of no particular moment whether political speech is dangerous, since political speech is by its nature often dangerous, or may often appear to be dangerous. This is because the free public use of our reason applies to the most fundamental questions, and the decisions made may have grave consequences. Suppose a democratic people, engaged in a military rivalry with an autocratic power, should decide that the use of nuclear weapons is so contrary to the principles of humanity that their use must be foresworn and significant steps taken unilaterally toward reducing these weapons, this done in the hope that the other power might be persuaded to follow. This could be a highly dangerous decision; but surely that is irrelevant to whether it should be freely discussed and whether the government is constitutionally obligated to carry out this decision once it is properly made. The dangerousness of political speech is beside the point; it is precisely the danger involved in making this decision which must be freely discussed. Wasn't it dangerous to hold free elections in 1862–64 in the midst of a civil war?

Focusing on the danger of political speech flawed the clear and present danger rule from the start. It failed to recognize that for free political speech to be restricted, a constitutional crisis must exist requiring the more or less temporary suspension of democratic political institutions, solely for the sake of preserving these institutions and other basic liberties. Such a crisis did not exist in 1862–64; and if not then, surely at no other time before or since. There was no constitutional crisis of the requisite kind when *Schenck*, *Debs*, or *Dennis* were decided, no political conditions which prevented free political institutions from operating. Never in our history has there been a time when free political speech, and in particular subversive advocacy, could be restricted or suppressed. And this suggests that in a country with a vigorous tradition of democratic institutions, a constitutional crisis need never arise unless its people and institutions are simply overwhelmed from the outside. For practical purposes, then, in a well-governed democratic society under reasonably favorable conditions, the free public use of our reason in questions of political and social justice would seem to be absolute.

Of course, the preceding remarks do not provide a systematic explanation of the distinction between a constitutional crisis of the requisite kind and an emergency in which there is a threat of serious injury, political, economic, and moral. I have simply appealed to the fact, or to what I take to be a fact, that we can recognize from a number of cases in our history that there is the distinction I have indicated and that often we can tell when it applies. Here I cannot go into a systematic explanation. I believe, however, that the notion of a constitutional crisis of this kind is an important part of an account of free political speech, and that when we explain this notion we must start from an account of free political speech which assigns it priority. In justice as fairness this kind of speech falls under the basic liberties, and while these liberties are not absolute, they can be restricted in their content (as opposed to being regulated in ways consistent with maintaining a fully adequate scheme) only if this is necessary to prevent a greater and more significant loss, either directly or indirectly, to these liberties. I have tried to illustrate how in the case of political speech, we try to identify the more essential elements in the central range of application of this basic liberty. We then proceed to further extensions up to the point where a fully adequate provision for this liberty is achieved, unless this liberty has already become self-limiting or conflicts with more significant extensions of other basic liberties. As always, I assume that these judgments are made by delegates and legislators from the point of view of the appropriate stage in the light of what best advances the rational interest of the representative equal citizen in a fully adequate scheme of basic liberties. If we insist on using the language of the clear and present danger rule, we must say, first, that the substantive evils which the legislature seeks to prevent must be of a highly special kind, namely, the loss of freedom of thought itself, or of other basic liberties, including here the fair-value of the political liberties; and second, that there must be no alternative way to prevent these evils than the restriction of free speech. This formulation of the rule goes with the requirement that a constitutional crisis of the requisite kind is one in which free political institutions cannot operate or take the steps required to preserve themselves.

XII

I now wish to supplement the preceding discussion of political speech in two ways. First, it needs to be emphasized that the basic liberties constitute a family, and that it is this family that has priority and not any single liberty by itself, even if, practically speaking, one or more of the basic liberties may be absolute under certain conditions. In this connection I shall very briefly note the manner in which political speech may be regulated in order to preserve the fair-value of the political liberties. I do this not, of course, to try to resolve this difficult problem, but to illustrate why the basic liberties need to be adjusted to one another and cannot be specified individually. Second, it is helpful in clarifying the notion of the basic liberties and their significance to survey several (non-basic) liberties associated with the second principle of justice. This serves to bring out how the significance of a liberty (whether basic or non-basic) is tied to its political and social role within a just basic structure as specified by the two principles of justice.

I begin in this section with the problem of maintaining the fair-value of the equal political liberties. Although (as I said in section VII) it is beyond the scope of a philosophical doctrine to consider in any detail how this problem is to be solved, such a doctrine must explain the grounds upon which the necessary institutions and rules of law can be justified. Let's assume, for reasons stated earlier, that public financing of political campaigns and election expenditures, various limits on contributions and other regulations are essential to maintain the fair-value of the political liberties.[70] These arrangements are compatible with the central role of free political speech and press as a basic liberty provided that the following three conditions hold. First, there are no restrictions on the content of speech; the arrangements in question are, therefore, regulations which favor no political doctrine over any other. They are, so to speak, rules of order for elections and are required to establish a just political procedure in which the fair-value of the equal political liberties is maintained.

A second condition is that the instituted arrangements must not impose any undue burdens on the various political groups in society and must affect them all in an equitable manner. Plainly, what counts as an undue burden is itself a question, and in any particular case is to be answered by reference to the purpose of achieving the fair-value of the political liberties. For example, the prohibition of large contributions from private persons or corporations to political candidates is not an undue burden (in the requisite sense) on wealthy persons and groups. Such a prohibition may be necessary so that citizens similarly gifted and motivated have roughly an equal chance of influencing the government's policy and of attaining positions of authority irrespective of their economic and social class. It is precisely this equality which defines the fair-value of the political liberties. On the other hand, regulations that restrict the use of certain public places for political speech might impose an undue burden on relatively poor groups

[70] See section VII.

accustomed to this way of conveying their views since they lack the funds for other kinds of political expression.

Finally, the various regulations of political speech must be rationally designed to achieve the fair-value of the political liberties. While it would be too strong to say that they must be the least restrictive regulations required to achieve this end — for who knows what the least restrictive among the equally effective regulations might be — nevertheless, these regulations become unreasonable once considerably less restrictive and equally effective alternatives are both known and available.

The point of the foregoing remarks is to illustrate how the basic liberties constitute a family, the members of which have to be adjusted to one another to guarantee the central range of these liberties in the two fundamental cases. Thus, political speech, even though it falls under the basic liberty of freedom of thought, must be regulated to insure the fair-value of the political liberties. These regulations do not restrict the content of political speech and hence may be consistent with its central role. It should be noted that the mutual adjustment of the basic liberties is justified on grounds allowed by the priority of these liberties as a family, no one of which is in itself absolute. This kind of adjustment is markedly different from a general balancing of interests which permits considerations of all kinds — political, economic, and social — to restrict these liberties, even regarding their content, when the advantages gained or injuries avoided are thought to be great enough. In justice as fairness the adjustment of the basic liberties is grounded solely on their significance as specified by their role in the two fundamental cases, and this adjustment is guided by the aim of specifying a fully adequate scheme of these liberties.

In the preceding two sections I recalled a part of development of doctrine from *Schenck* to *Brandenburg*, a development with a happy ending. By contrast, *Buckley* and its sequel *First National*

Bank are profoundly dismaying.[71] In *Buckley* the Court held unconstitutional various limits on expenditures imposed by the Election Act Amendment of 1974. These limits applied to expenditures in favor of individual candidates, to expenditures by candidates from their own funds, and to total expenditures in the course of a campaign. The Court said that the First Amendment cannot tolerate such provisions since they place direct and substantial restrictions on political speech.[72] For the most part the Court considers what it regards as the primary government interest served by the Act, namely, the interest in preventing corruption of the electoral process, and the appearance of such corruption. The Court also considers two so-called ancillary interests of the Act, namely, the interest in limiting the increasing costs of political campaigns and the interest in equalizing the relative ability of citizens to affect the outcome of elections. Here I am concerned solely with the legitimacy of this second ancillary interest, since it is the only one which falls directly under the notion of the fair-value of the political liberties. Moreover, I leave aside, as irrelevant for our purposes, the question whether the measures enacted by Congress were rationally framed to fulfill this interest in an effective way.

---

[71] Buckley v. Valeo, 424 U.S. 1 (1976), and First National Bank v. Bellotti, 435 U.S. 765 (1978). For discussions of *Buckley*, see Tribe, *American Constitutional Law*, ch. 13, pp. 800–11; and Skelly Wright, "Political Speech and the Constitution: Is Money Speech?," *Yale Law Journal*, vol. 85, no. 8 (July 1976), pp. 1001–21. For an earlier discussion, see M. A. Nicholson, "Campaign Financing and Equal Protection," *Stanford Law Review*, vol. 26 (April 1974), pp. 815–54. In *First National Bank* the Court, by a 5 to 4 decision, invalidated a Massachusetts criminal law which prohibited expenditures by banks and corporations for the purpose of influencing the outcome of voting on referendum proposals, unless these proposals materially affected the property, business, or assets of the corporation. The statute specified that no referendum question solely concerning the taxation of individuals came under this exception. In a dissent joined by Brennan and Marshall, Justice White said that the fundamental error of the majority opinion was its failure to recognize that the government's interest in prohibiting such expenditures by banks and corporations derives from the First Amendment — in particular, from the value of promoting free political discussion by preventing corporate domination; see 435 U.S. 765 (1978) at 803–4. My discussion in the text is in sympathy with this dissenting opinion, and also with White's dissent in *Buckley* at 257–66, and with Marshall's at 287–90.

[72] Buckley v. Valeo, at 58–59.

What is dismaying is that the present Court seems to reject altogether the idea that Congress may try to establish the fairvalue of the political liberties. It says: "the concept that the government may restrict the speech of some elements in our society in order to enhance the relative voice of others is wholly foreign to the First Amendment." [73] The Court then proceeds to cite its own precedents, holding that the First Amendment was designed to secure the widest possible dissemination of information from diverse and opposed sources, and to assure the unrestricted exchange of ideas for bringing about political and social changes favored by the people. [74] But none of the cases cited involves the fundamental question of the fair-value of the political liberties. [75] Moreover, the Court's opinion focuses too much on the so-called primary interest in eliminating corruption and the appearance of corruption. The Court fails to recognize the essential point that the fair-value of the political liberties is required for a just political procedure, and that to insure their fair-value it is necessary to prevent those with greater property and wealth, and the greater skills of organization which accompany them, from controlling the electoral process to their advantage. The way in which this is accomplished need not involve bribery and dishonesty or the granting of special favors, however common these vices may be. Shared political convictions and aims suffice. In *Buckley* the Court runs the risk of endorsing the view that fair representation is representation according to the amount of influence effectively exerted. On this view, democracy is a kind of regulated rivalry between economic classes and interest groups in which the outcome should properly depend on the ability and willingness of each to use its financial resources and skills, admittedly very unequal, to make its desires felt.

[73] Ibid., at 48–49.

[74] Ibid., at 49–51.

[75] See Tribe, *American Constitutional Law*, p. 806.

It is surprising, however, that the Court should think that attempts by Congress to establish the fair-value of the political liberties must run afoul of the First Amendment. In a number of earlier decisions the Court has affirmed the principle of one person, one vote, sometimes relying on Article I, Section 2 of the Constitution, at other times on the Fourteenth Amendment. It has said of the right to vote that it is the "preservative of all rights," and in *Wesberry* it stated: "Other rights, even the most basic, are illusory if the right to vote is undermined." [76] In *Reynolds* the Court recognized that this right involves more than the right simply to cast a vote which is counted equally. The Court said: "Full and effective participation by all citizens in state government requires . . . that each citizen has an equally effective voice in the election of members of the state legislature." [77] Later in the opinion it said: "Since achieving of fair and effective representation for all citizens is concededly the basic aim of legislative apportionment, we conclude that the Equal Protection Clause guarantees the opportunity for equal participation by voters in the election of state legislators." [78] Thus, what is fundamental is a political procedure which secures for all citizens a full and equally effective voice in a fair scheme of representation. Such a scheme is fundamental because the adequate protection of other basic rights depends on it. Formal equality is not enough.

It would seem to follow that the aim of achieving a fair scheme of representation can justify limits on and regulations of political speech in elections, provided that these limits and regulations satisfy the three conditions mentioned earlier. For how else is the full and effective voice of all citizens to be maintained? Since it is a matter of one basic liberty against another, the liberties protected by the First Amendment may have to be adjusted

[76] Wesberry v. Sanders, 376 U.S. 1 (1964) at 17.
[77] Reynolds v. Sims, 377 U.S. 533 (1964) at 565.
[78] Ibid., at 565–66.

in the light of other constitutional requirements, in this case the requirement of the fair-value of the political liberties. Not to do so is to fail to see a constitution as a whole and to fail to recognize how its provisions are to be taken together in specifying a just political procedure as an essential part of a fully adequate scheme of basic liberties.

As already noted (in section VII), what kinds of electoral arrangements are required to establish the fair-value of the political liberties is an extremely difficult question. It is not the task of the Court to say what these arrangements are, but to make sure that the arrangements enacted by the legislature accord with the Constitution. The regulations proposed by Congress and struck down in *Buckley* would quite possibly have been ineffective; but in the present state of our knowledge they were admissible attempts to achieve the aim of a fair scheme of representation in which all citizens could have a more full and effective voice. If the Court means what it says in *Wesberry* and *Reynolds*, *Buckley* must sooner or later give way. The First Amendment no more enjoins a system of representation according to influence effectively exerted in free political rivalry between unequals than the Fourteenth Amendment enjoins a system of liberty of contract and free competition between unequals in the economy, as the Court thought in the Lochner era.[79] In both cases the results of the free play of the electoral process and of economic competition are acceptable only if the necessary conditions of background justice are fulfilled. Moreover, in a democratic regime it is important that the fulfillment of these conditions be publicly recognized. This is more fundamental than avoiding corruption and the appearance of corruption; for without the public recognition that background justice is maintained, citizens tend to become resentful, cynical, and apathetic. It is this state of mind that leads to corruption as a serious problem, and indeed makes it uncontrollable. The danger of

[79] Lochner v. New York, 198 U.S. 45 (1905).

Buckley is that it risks repeating the mistake of the Lochner era, this time in the political sphere where, for reasons the Court itself has stated in the cases cited above, the mistake could be much more grievous.

XIII

To clarify further the notion of the significance of the basic liberties I shall briefly discuss several liberties associated with the second principle of justice. The examples I consider are related to advertising; and although some of these liberties are quite important, they are not basic liberties, since they do not have the requisite role and significance in the two fundamental cases.

We may distinguish three kinds of advertising according to whether the information conveyed concerns political questions, openings for jobs and positions, or the nature of products for sale. Political advertising I shall not discuss; I assume that it can be regulated for the reasons just considered in the preceding section, provided that the regulations in question satisfy the conditions already indicated. Let us turn, then, to advertisements of openings for jobs and positions. These contain information important in maintaining fair equality of opportunity. Since the first part of the second principle of justice requires that social and economic inequalities are to be attached to offices and positions open to everyone under conditions of fair equality of opportunity, this kind of advertising is associated with this part of the principle and it is granted protection accordingly. Thus, announcements of jobs and positions can be forbidden to contain statements which exclude applicants of certain designated ethnic and racial groups, or of either sex, when these limitations are contrary to fair equality of opportunity. The notion of fair equality of opportunity, like that of a basic liberty, has a central range of application which consists of various liberties together with certain conditions under which these liberties can be effectively exercised. The advertising of employment opportunities may be restricted and regulated to

preserve intact this central range. Just as in the case of basic
liberties, I assume that this range of application can be preserved
in ways consistent with the other requirements of justice, and in
particular with the basic liberties. Observe here that the restrictions in question, in contrast with the basic liberties, may be restrictions on content.

In the case of the advertising of products, let's distinguish two
kinds. The first kind is advertising which contains information
about prices and the features of products used by knowledgeable
purchasers as criteria of evaluation. Assuming that the two principles of justice are best satisfied by a substantial use of a system
of free competitive markets, economic policy should encourage
this kind of advertising. This is true whether the economy is that
of a private-property democracy or a liberal socialist regime. In
order for markets to be workably competitive and efficient, it is
necessary for consumers to be well informed about both prices and
the relevant features of available products. The law may impose
penalties for inaccurate or false information, which it cannot do
in the case of freedom of thought and liberty of conscience; and
for the protection of consumers the law can require that information about harmful and dangerous properties of goods be clearly
described on the label, or in some other suitable manner. In addition, it may be forbidden for firms, or for trade and professional
associations, to make agreements to limit or not to engage in this
kind of advertising. The legislature may require, for example, that
prices and accurate information about commodities be readily
accessible to the public. Such measures help to maintain a competitive and efficient system of markets and enable consumers to
make more intelligent and informed decisions.

A second kind of advertising of products is market-strategic
advertising, which is found in imperfect and oligopolistic markets
dominated by relatively few firms. Here the aim of a firm's expenditures on advertising may be either aggressive, for example,
to expand its volume of sales or its share of the market; or the

aim may be defensive: firms may be forced to advertise in order to preserve their position in the industry. In these cases consumers are usually unable to distinguish between the products of firms except by rather superficial and unimportant properties; advertising tries to influence consumers' preferences by presenting the firm as trustworthy through the use of slogans, eye-catching photographs, and so on, all designed to form or to strengthen the habit of buying the firm's products. Much of this kind of advertising is socially wasteful, and a well-ordered society that tries to preserve competition and to remove market imperfections would seek reasonable ways to limit it. The funds now devoted to advertising can be released for investment or for other useful social ends. Thus, the legislature might, for example, encourage agreements among firms to limit expenditures on this kind of advertising through taxes and by enforcing such contracts as legally valid. I am not concerned here with how practicable such a policy would be, but solely with illustrating how in this case the right to advertise, which is a kind of speech, can be restricted by contract, and therefore this right is not inalienable, in contrast to the basic liberties.

I must digress a moment to explain this last point. To say that the basic liberties are inalienable is to say that any agreement by citizens which waives or violates a basic liberty, however rational and voluntary this agreement may be, is void *ab initio*; that is, it has no legal force and does not affect any citizen's basic liberties. Moreover, the priority of the basic liberties implies that they cannot be justly denied to any one, or to any group of persons, or even to all citizens generally, on the grounds that such is the desire, or overwhelming preference, of an effective political majority, however strong and enduring. The priority of liberty excludes such considerations from the grounds that can be entertained.

A common-sense explanation of why the basic liberties are inalienable might say, following an idea of Montesquieu, that the

basic liberties of each citizen are a part of public liberty, and
therefore in a democratic state a part of sovereignty. The Constitution specifies a just political procedure in accordance with
which this sovereignty is exercised subject to limits which guarantee the integrity of the basic liberties of each citizen. Thus
agreements which alienate these liberties cannot be enforced by
law, which consists of but enactments of sovereignty. Montesquieu
believed that to sell one's status as a citizen (and, let's add, any
part of it) is an act so extravagant that we cannot attribute it to
anyone. He thought that its value to the seller must be beyond all
price.[80] In justice as fairness, the sense in which this is so can be
explained as follows. We use the original position to model the
conception of free and equal persons as both reasonable and
rational, and then the parties as rationally autonomous representatives of such persons select the two principles of justice which
guarantee the basic liberties and their priority. The grounds upon
which the parties are moved to guarantee these liberties, together
with the constraints of the Reasonable, explain why the basic
liberties are, so to speak, beyond all price to persons so conceived.
For these liberties are beyond all price to the representatives of
citizens as free and equal persons when these representatives adopt
principles of justice for the basic structure in the original position.
The aims and conduct of citizens in society are therefore subordinate to the priority of these liberties, and thus in effect subordinate
to the conception of citizens as free and equal persons.

This explanation of why the basic liberties are inalienable does
not exclude the possibility that even in a well-ordered society some
citizens may want to circumscribe or alienate one or more of their
basic liberties. They may promise to vote for a certain political
party or candidate; or they may enter into a relationship with a
party or candidate such that it is a breach of trust not to vote in a
certain way. Again, members of a religious association may regard

[80] *The Spirit of the Laws*, B 15, ch. 2.

themselves as having submitted in conscience to religious authority, and therefore as not free, from the standpoint of that relationship, to question its pronouncements. Relationships of this
kind are obviously neither forbidden nor in general improper.[81]

The essential point here is that the conception of citizens as
free and equal persons is not required in a well-ordered society as
a personal or associational or moral ideal (see section III, first
paragraph). Rather it is a political conception affirmed for the
sake of establishing an effective public conception of justice. Thus
the institutions of the basic structure do not enforce undertakings
which waive or limit the basic liberties. Citizens are always at
liberty to vote as they wish and to change their religious affiliations. This, of course, protects their liberty to do things which they
regard, or which they may come to regard, as wrong, and which
indeed may be wrong. (Thus, they are at liberty to break promises
to vote in a certain way, or to apostatize.) This is not a contradic-
tion but simply a consequence of the role of the basic liberties in
this political conception of justice.

After this digression, we can sum up by saying that the protection for different kinds of advertising varies depending on whether
it is connected with political speech, or with maintaining fair
equality of opportunity, or with preserving a workably competitive
and efficient system of markets. The conception of the person in
justice as fairness ascribes to the self a capacity for a certain
hierarchy of interests; and this hierarchy is expressed by the nature
of the original position (for example, by the way the Reasonable
frames and subordinates the Rational) and by the priorities in the
two principles of justice. The second principle of justice is subordinate to the first since the first guarantees the basic liberties

---

[81] There are many other reasons why citizens in certain situations or at certain
times might not put much value on the exercise of some of their basic liberties and
might want to do an action which limited these liberties in various ways. Unless these
possibilities affect the agreement of the parties in the original position (and I hold that
they do not), they are irrelevant to the inalienability of the basic liberties. I am indebted to Arthur Kuflik for discussion on this point.

required for the full and informed exercise of the two moral powers in the two fundamental cases. The role of the second principle of justice is to ensure fair equality of opportunity and to regulate the social and economic system so that social resources are properly used and the means to citizens' ends are produced efficiently and fairly shared. Of course, this division of role between the two principles of justice is but part of a guiding framework for deliberation; nevertheless, it brings out why the liberties associated with the second principles are less significant in a well-ordered society than the basic liberties secured by the first.

XIV

I conclude with several comments. First, I should emphasize that the discussion of free speech in the last four sections is not intended to advance any of the problems that actually face constitutional jurists. My aim has been solely to illustrate how the basic liberties are specified and adjusted to one another in the application of the two principles of justice. The conception of justice to which these principles belong is not to be regarded as a method of answering the jurist's questions, but as a guiding framework, which if jurists find it convincing, may orient their reflections, complement their knowledge, and assist their judgment. We must not ask too much of a philosophical view. A conception of justice fulfills its social role provided that persons equally conscientious and sharing roughly the same beliefs find that, by affirming the framework of deliberation set up by it, they are normally led to a sufficient convergence of judgment necessary to achieve effective and fair social cooperation. My discussion of the basic liberties and their priority should be seen in this light.

In this connection recall that the conception of justice as fairness is addressed to that impasse in our recent political history shown in the lack of agreement on the way basic institutions are to be arranged if they are to conform to the freedom and equality of citizens as persons. Thus justice as fairness is addressed not so much to constitutional jurists as to citizens in a constitutional regime. It presents a way for them to conceive of their common and guaranteed status as equal citizens and attempts to connect a particular understanding of freedom and equality with a particular conception of the person thought to be congenial to the shared notions and essential convictions implicit in the public culture of a democratic society. Perhaps in this way the impasse concerning the understanding of freedom and equality can at least be intellectually clarified if not resolved. It is particularly important to keep in mind that the conception of the person is part of a conception of political and social justice. That is, it characterizes how citizens are to think of themselves and of one another in their political and social relationships, and, therefore, as having the basic liberties appropriate to free and equal persons capable of being fully cooperating members of society over a complete life. The role of a conception of the person in a conception of political justice is distinct from its role in a personal or associational ideal, or in a religious or moral way of life. The basis of toleration and of social cooperation on a footing of mutual respect in a democratic regime is put in jeopardy when these distinctions are not recognized; for when this happens and such ideals and ways of life take a political form, the fair-terms of cooperation are narrowly drawn, and free and willing cooperation between persons with different conceptions of the good may become impossible. In this lecture I have tried to strengthen the liberal view (as a philosophical doctrine) by indicating how the basic liberties and their priority belong to the fair-terms of cooperation between citizens who regard themselves and one another according to a conception of free and equal persons.

Finally, an observation about the concluding paragraphs of Hart's essay to which my discussion owes so much. Hart is quite rightly unconvinced by the grounds explicitly offered in *A Theory of Justice* for the priority of the basic liberties. He suggests that the apparently dogmatic course of my argument for this priority may be explained by my tacitly imputing to the parties in the original position a latent ideal of my own. This latent ideal, he thinks, is that of a public-spirited citizen who prizes political activity and service to others so highly that the exchange of the opportunities for such activities for mere material good and contentment would be rejected. Hart goes on to say that this ideal is, of course, one of the main ideals of liberalism; but the difficulty is that my argument for "the priority of liberty purports to rest on interests, not on ideals, and to demonstrate that the general priority of liberty reflects a preference for liberty over other goods which every self-interested person who is rational would have." [82] Now Hart is correct in saying that the priority of liberty cannot be argued for by imputing this ideal of the person to the parties in the original position; and he is right also in supposing that a conception of the person in some sense liberal underlies the argument for the priority of liberty. But this conception is the altogether different conception of citizens as free and equal persons; and it does not enter justice as fairness by imputation to the parties. Rather, it enters through the constraints of the Reasonable imposed on the parties in the original position as well as in the revised account of primary goods. This conception of the person as free and equal also appears in the recognition by the parties that the persons they represent have the two moral powers and a certain psychological nature. How these elements lead to the basic liberties and their priority is sketched in sections V and VI, and there the deliberations of the parties were rational and based on the determinate good of the persons represented. This conception of the person can be said to be liberal (in the sense of the philosophical doctrine) because it takes the capacity for social cooperation as fundamental and attributes to persons the two moral powers which make such cooperation possible. These powers specify the basis of equality. Thus citizens

[82] Hart, p. 555. Daniels, p. 252.

are regarded as having a certain natural political virtue without which the hopes for a regime of liberty may be unrealistic. Moreover, persons are assumed to have different and incommensurable conceptions of the good so that the unity of social cooperation rests on a public conception of justice which secures the basic liberties. Yet despite this plurality of conceptions of the good, the notion of society as a social union of social unions shows how it is possible to coordinate the benefits of human diversity into a more comprehensive good.

While the grounds I have surveyed for the basic liberties and their priority have been drawn from and develop considerations found in *A Theory of Justice*, I failed to bring them together in that work. Furthermore, the grounds I cited for this priority were not sufficient, and in some cases even incompatible with the kind of doctrine I was trying to work out.[83] I hope that the argument in this lecture is an improvement, thanks to Hart's critical discussion.

---

[83] Here I refer to the errors in paragraphs 3–4 of section 82 of *TJ*, the section in which the grounds for the priority of liberty are discussed explicitly. Two main errors are first, that I did not enumerate the most important grounds in a clear way; and second, in paragraph 3, pp. 542–43, that I should not have used the notion of the diminishing marginal significance of economic and social advantages relative to our interest in the basic liberties, which interest is said to become stronger as the social conditions for effectively exercising these liberties are more fully realized. Here the notion of marginal significance is incompatible with the notion of a hierarchy of interests used in par. 4, p. 543. It is this latter notion, founded on a certain conception of the person as a free and equal person, which is required by a Kantian view. The marginal changes I could have spoken of in par. 3 are the marginal, or step-by-step, changes reflected in the gradual realization of the social conditions which are necessary for the full and effective exercise of the basic liberties. But these changes are a different matter altogether from the marginal significance of interests.

Is Liberty Possible?

CHARLES FRIED

THE TANNER LECTURES ON HUMAN VALUES

Delivered at
Stanford University

May 14 and 18, 1981

CHARLES FRIED was born in Czechoslovakia in 1935, received his A.B. degree from Princeton University and M.A. in Jurisprudence from the University of Oxford. His J.D. degree is from Columbia Law School. After serving as law clerk to Justice John Marshall Harlan of the U.S. Supreme Court in 1960–61, he began teaching at Harvard Law School, where he was Carter Professor of General Jurisprudence until 1985, when he became Solicitor General of the United States. His books are *An Anatomy of Values* (1970); *Medical Experimentation: Personal Integrity and Social Policy* (1974); *Right and Wrong* (1978); and *Contract as Promise: A Theory of Contractual Obligation* (1981).

I am grateful to the Trustees of the Tanner Lectures on Human Values and the University of Utah Press for allowing me to combine in this one essay what were originally two lectures, both delivered at Stanford University in May 1981. The second of these, appearing as Part II here, is part of a continuing project on the foundations of private law, assisted by a summer research grant from the Harvard Law School and a grant from the Olin Foundation. In addition to those who commented on these lectures in Stanford — I think especially of Patrick Atiyah, Wayne Barnett, Mitchell Polinsky, Thomas Scanlon, Alan Stone, and Steven Strasnik — I received valuable comments from Sissela Bok, John Ely, Frank Michelman, Richard Parker, William Ewald, Judith Jarvis Thomson, and the members of SELF to whom I presented a preliminary draft. Hilary Putnam was particularly generous in sharing his time, ideas, and an early draft of his Reason, Truth and History *(Cambridge University Press, 1981).*

* * *

PART I. FAIR SHARES — THE SEARCH FOR A STANDARD

1. Is liberty possible? The question is intended both in a practical and philosophical sense. The practical question is can we devise institutions which express a commitment to individual liberty while fulfilling the other imperatives of social ethics, particularly the claims which the unequal enjoyment of resources or outcomes make on the better favored and thus on the community as a whole. The related philosophical question asks whether there is a coherent concept of liberty at all. The questions tie together in this way. If the situation of individuals depends on collective claims for contribution to the well-being of others, that situation

is insecure and their liberty is threatened. If the very definition or conception of what a person's situation is depends on collective claims directed at collective goals, including collective goals about fair distribution, the distinctness of the concept of liberty is undermined. To put the issues crudely at the outset, if everything about an individual — his person or his product — is available for redistribution, then individuals are not free. And if there is not even any stable way to define what a person's entitlements or rights are before we proceed to consider redistributing, if the very conception of what are my resources such that I must make contribution from them inevitably touches on issues of collective and redistributive goals, then liberty is not possible in the deep, philosophical sense. It is not an independent concept at all.

The first of these questions, the question of fair shares or distributive justice is a staple of political philosophy. The most complete recent attempt to argue for a conception of fair shares, John Rawls's *A Theory of Justice*, sets the standard for debate on this subject. In an earlier work[1] I objected that Rawls's celebrated maximin proposal is ambiguous about the extent to which a person's talent, ambition, character are or are not social assets only provisionally assigned by the morally irrelevant hazard of what he calls the natural lottery. To the extent that maximin allows the better endowed to hold out for higher income in exchange for their contribution to the situation of the worst-off, it seems to recognize a moral title in those endowments after all. But if there is such a moral title, then one wonders how an obligation to contribute what is one's own arises at all. Rawls's suggestion that the better endowed are indeed entitled to enjoy the fruits of their greater endowments but only to the extent that this improves the situation of the least well-off hardly lays these doubts to rest, but rather just restates the initial proposition.

[1] *Right and Wrong*, 161n (Cambridge, Mass., 1978); C. Fried, review of *A Theory of Justice*, 85 Harv. L. Rev. (1972).

The second of my questions, about the coherence of the concept of liberty, arises in the midst of the first, for both Rawls and a critic of Rawls such as Nozick assume that there is some clear sense to the notions of what is attributable to a person, what are his endowments.[2] They assume a conception of property in one's person, one's talents and efforts, and a conception of property in the fruits of those talents and efforts. Indeed, as I intend to show in detail in Part II, what both Rawls and a critic such as Nozick need are stable conceptions of tort and contract — that is, notions about how and what interests deserve recognition and protection and how far one may dispose of or exchange what is one's own. Such a stable basis is necessary so that we can make sense out of the question of how much of what is attributable to a person should be left with him and how much exacted by way of contribution to the well-being of others. But there is a critique which holds that there is no defensible way to resolve that subsequent question except by attending explicitly to distributive and other collective goals.[3] For instance, a transfer induced by fraud should not be allowed to stand and the victim of the fraud should have his property returned to him. This seems like a judgment which has nothing to do with distribution — it is pre-distributive, a part of a system of rights on which the distributive judgment works. Yet what is a fraud is a question which itself seems to implicate distributive judgments: how far may one profit from greater shrewdness, how far must one share information which bears on the desirability of a bargain? If liberty is threatened by the spectre of redistribution, which subjects me and what is mine to the needs of others, how much more is liberty threatened if we cannot even tell what is mine without considering those claims.

[2] John Rawls, *A Theory of Justice*, ch. 5 (Cambridge, Mass., 1971); Robert Nozick, *Anarchy, State and Utopia*, ch. 7 (New York, 1974).

[3] See, e.g., Kennedy and Michelman, "Are Property and Contract Efficient?" 8 *Hofstra L. Rev.* 711 (1980); Kronman, "Contract Law and Distributive Justice," 89 *Yale L. J.* 472 (1980).

Thus the two themes of fair shares and private rights connect. The first belongs to political philosophy, the second to legal theory, but both are necessary to a conception of liberty. And they seem to chase each other in a circle: distribution presupposes a system of private rights, and yet no such system seems available without settling distributive issues. So there is not only a set of substantive issues to be resolved, but an epistemological or methodological issue as well — how to cut into this circle. That should not be a surprise, for it has always been objected that liberty is a meaningless concept without the specification of the very social background which liberty is supposed to judge and constrain. I shall proceed by asking first in a general way why we should be concerned about liberty and about distribution. Then I shall propose and define a standard of distribution, ignoring provisionally the problems of legal theory which threaten the coherence of the terms in that proposal. In Part II I confront these, showing how we may hope for a theory of private rights. Along the way I hope to illuminate the methodological concern that any conception of liberty must try to jump out of its own conceptual skin, which of course it cannot do.

2. It is well to say in a simple way at the outset why I care about liberty and what I fear about redistributive and other collective claims that seem to threaten liberty. Though it may seem an irony in a statement which announces a desire to remain simple, the shortest way is to describe my orientation as Kantian. I do not know of a standard of value beyond man, and I know of nothing about man more valuable than his capacity to reflect about how his life should be lived, and to act on the conclusion of those reflections. This is a simple rendering of what Kant meant when he called man a moral being and defined moral nature as free and rational. Each person's judgment finally is his own — there can be no conclusions about truth or right for him unless he attains conviction about them. From this follows a sense of responsibility. A man is responsible for his own judgments because they express

his moral personality, the exercise of his rational capacities — they are his. He is responsible for what he becomes because he chooses a conception of the good and lives according to it. And he is responsible for what he does in the world and for what he does to others, because the life he chooses and is responsible for is lived in the world among other people. And so in this most basic way we are separate, even lonely beings, choosing alone and responsible as we choose.

Kant speaks of rational beings, but the only moral beings we know are embodied human beings, with physical needs and capacities which correlate with or support the moral capacities. The happiness a man or woman seeks is the happiness which can be attained by a rational animal. The biological individual is the atomic unit of this system, just as the discrete consciousness is the atomic unit of the more abstract system of rational morality. Liberty is just the recognition of this moral status of flesh and blood men and women — each separate, each responsible to himself for the judgments he makes and the life he chooses.

Collective claims are a threat to this conception of liberty. Collective claims by definition are claims by the many, so that a lone individual lacks the brute power to resist them. At worst they can overwhelm an individual's efforts to live his life according to his judgment and choices. At best he may be fortunate enough to belong to a coalition which shares his vision. Most likely he will have to compromise that vision in order to be part of a successful coalition. Now the prospect of joining successful coalitions improves one's prospects of attaining his goals, but only by imposing those goals on others — in Kant's phrase, by using others as a means to one's ends. Thus coalitions are compromises in which we are partially overwhelmed and partially seek to overwhelm others. The principle of liberty resolves these conflicts by allowing each individual to choose his own life, neither imposed on nor imposing on others. Cooperation in achieving one's ends must be completely voluntary on the part of each collaborator. The non-imposition or conservative aspect of liberty is expressed in the law of torts; the cooperative or creative aspect in the law of contracts.

Now may not an individual's effort to live his life and realize his conception of the good be overwhelmed as well by natural circumstances as by the claims of others, and does it not hurt as much one way as the other? Implicit in my position is the assumption that it hurts more and in a different way to be consumed by the state than to be consumed by a tiger. This assumption is captured by the usual definition of coercion as subjection to the power of another person, and liberty as the absence of coercion. The law of gravity does not coerce us. Coercion and its correlative concept, liberty, define a relation between persons, a relation specified by the principles persons may be taken to adopt to justify the way they treat each other. Thus, for instance, a claim to compel contribution of a man's above-average talents implies an appeal to the principle that talents are social property. The tiger, however, takes no stand on the moral worth or defining characteristics of the person he devours. His action has no maxim. And thus a man's liberty is not threatened — though his welfare may be — by drought, sickness, or the prevalence of tigers. A thief, extortionist, or demagogue threatens liberty directly.

3. I shall now offer as simple a ground for redistribution — for the claim that others make on us for our sharing and sacrifice. As other persons share our moral worth, as they have lives which it is of consuming importance to them that they be able to live out according to their conception, as they are for this reason beyond price (or in an older language, as they have souls), it is wrong for us to be indifferent to them. The success and happiness of my fellow men and women cannot be indifferent to me unless I would deny the moral worth of my own projects and my freedom to pursue them. Human misery is but the helpless sense that what you value above all is slipping irreversibly out of your grasp. And to proclaim indifference as one's principle in the face of the misery of others is inconsistent with proclaiming the moral worth of one's

own happiness. This is, I think, the true meaning of Kant's argument for a duty of beneficence in the fourth example in the *Grundlegung.*[4] And just as law and a formal system of property are the ways in which the principles of liberty and of man's imperium over nature find expression in the world, so systems of taxation and redistribution express in modern social circumstances a part of our duty of beneficence, a part of our duty to have regard for the misery of others.

What standard of distribution does this conception entail? In *Right and Wrong* I sought to avoid that question by positing a generalized right to a fair share of the community's scarce resources, leaving open what the specification of that share should be: an equal share, or a maximin share, or one where the top did not exceed some multiple of the bottom, or the bottom did not fall below some fraction of the mean.[5] My concern there was to argue what the fair share was a share of: scarce resources as measured by their market price, that is, demand for them relative to their scarcity. I was anxious to exclude persons, their talents and abilities from that levy. I sought to make plain that the attempt was not to arrive at some fair proportion (equality or whatever) in the attainment of relative happiness, which rather it was the individual's responsibility to construct out of his fair share. Nor yet was it an attempt to satisfy needs as distinguished from wants, since these might be met by what I called the insurance principle, the premiums being paid out of one's fair share. But I doubt today if one can separate the incidence of the tax, what it falls on, from its rate, how progressive it should be. What the rate is will make a crucial difference to how significant an intrusion is authorized. A low rate levied on everything, even talents, would be much less significant than a high rate levied just on external goods.

[4] *Foundations of the Metaphysics of Morals* 41[424], Lewis White Beck trans. (Indianapolis, 1959).

[5] *Supra*, note 1, at chs. 5, 6.

And the concept of fair shares itself implies a prima facie standard of distribution: equality.

In my earlier treatment I sought to avoid this inevitable pressure toward equality by limiting the incidence of the tax to external resources, thus affirmatively excluding a man's earning *potential.* This point was further made by following Rawls in suggesting that the tax be a consumption tax. Of course one may ask whether leisure should be classed as a form of consumption, or whether working at an occupation returning less than one's highest available wage is a form of leisure, or whether and when personal services constitute a form of leisure/consumption. And thus arise again all the questions about measuring a man's share of scarce resources versus his own personal characteristics. The talk of fair share of scarce (external) resources assumes a picture, as Robert Nozick has argued, of people coming upon a stock of goods (manna from heaven) which must be shared out — fairly.[6] But as Nozick's own discussion demonstrated, the stock of goods in the actual world is so inextricably bound up with the efforts of those who have identified or transformed them that there seems little hope of finding a way of separating out what portion of a man's income or consumption is attributable to his efforts and what to the unworked store of natural external goods.

The same conclusion of hopelessness is forced on us from another angle. If equality is indeed the standard — perhaps only equality of external scarce resources — how are we to avoid constant interference? For as men and women of varying talents, dispositions, interests, and luck consumed, wasted, gave away, exchanged, ventured, and invested their resources and efforts significant departures from equality would soon arise. These departures would either have to be tolerated and equality therefore abandoned or frequent corrections made, which would, however, render impossible the investment and effort which the conception

---

[6] *Supra*, note 2, at 198, 219.

of liberty and responsibility for one's own life requires. Ronald
Dworkin has argued recently that: (1) Equality is compatible
with the kind of ex post inequality which results from the varying
outcomes of individual risk-taking, provided there was equality
initially; and (2) bad luck in risk-taking and bad luck in failing
to have talents and personal characteristics which command a high
rent in a particular social situation may both be assimilated to the
bad luck of handicap or illness. As we can imagine individuals
insuring against the bad luck of illness so also they may be
imagined as insuring against bad luck in investments and more
strikingly against the bad luck of being less talented than the
mean.[7] Thus is ex post inequality squared with ex ante equality.
The proposal is ingenious since it allows a considerable degree of
actual inequality while proclaiming continued allegiance to the
standard of equality which fair shares seems to require. (In this it
resembles Rawls's maximin.) Unfortunately the application of
the standard to actual social circumstances must proceed by way
of a rather elaborate thought experiment about what level of
premium individuals ignorant of their own economic rent would
be willing to pay to obtain up to what level of insurance. As in
the case of Rawls's original position, this thought experiment may
be used to conceal or to display substantive moral judgments necessary to its operation. And again as with the original position the
question arises, once the substantive moral judgments have been
displayed, whether these would not have sufficed to answer our
practical moral concerns directly.

I would prefer to return directly to the Kantian basis for distribution which I have announced: a sympathetic concern by each
for each, a moral imperative to avoid indifference in the face of a
fellow man's misery — as I have defined misery. This basis (unlike
talk of fair shares) in no way suggests equality as a prima facie

---

[7] "What Is Equality? Part 2: Equality of Resources," 10 *Philosophy and Public
Affairs* 283 (1981).

standard of distribution. Indeed distribution and fair shares are themselves not implied by it, for there is no commitment to a picture of things being shared out at all. My basis is quite compatible with the argument that there is no way of distinguishing between external goods and those which have been transformed by individual and collective effort and appropriation. There is no need to distinguish between good luck in investments and good luck in the economic rent of one's talents and characteristics. It is the need, the misery itself which makes its claim, and that misery and the steps toward its alleviation can be evaluated from the actual situation in which we find ourselves. There is no necessity of appealing to any hypothetical lotteries, auctions, contracts, or insurance policies.

4. If the claims of others are to accommodate liberty, those claims must be clearly defined and limited, and those limits must leave the individual a significant private sphere to live his life. Does the basis for redistribution I have just identified — sympathetic response to the misery of another — do more than announce a sentimentality which lacks any definite promise of substantive help or for that matter any limits to the claim for help? I shall suggest that it may do both to a sufficient degree. And by the way my proposal should explain as well why a proper conception of liberty and distributive justice, given suitable background conditions, requires no demonstration that the original historical acquisition of holdings was itself legitimate. It is sufficient that we have a just system of private law — that is, one which recognizes property and personal rights in the law of tort and contract — a democratic government, and appropriate redistributive mechanisms.

What is a man due? I would say these things: First, so much of the community's resources that he has a chance to live decently and to make a life for himself — by his own efforts if possible, by the community's aid if those efforts are insufficient. Beyond that he should demand nothing. Beyond that to use political power to demand more is to violate the liberty of his fellows. How and in terms of what is this social minimum to be determined?

This is my proposal: *A person has a claim on his fellows to a standard package of basic or essential goods — housing, education, health care, food: i.e., the social (or decent) minimum — if by reasonable efforts he cannot earn enough to procure this minimum for himself.*

To fix the level of enjoyment of the components of the social minimum, suppose: a state which for a substantial period has enjoyed normal democratic institutions: free expression, legislatures, elections — in short, a standard liberal democratic regime. In that state certain levels of essential goods and services will have been achieved. A long period of wide political participation and reasonably regular and stable institutions are hardly conceivable otherwise. This general distribution of basic goods is both a necessary condition for and an inevitable result of a reasonably long tenure of the kinds of institutions I am positing. Of course this leaves much open about the details of the pattern of distribution. There may be a small group with very large wealth. The lower income classes, say some unskilled workers, may exist in conditions of hardship and uncertainty. Also, there may be pockets of real misery. These may implicate the victims of past or continuing practices which under any conception of democratic theory must be taken as unjust. Or they may be the victims of dislocations, misfortunes, or circumstances not created by the government itself. Examples would be workers in sectors depressed by changing economic circumstances, recent immigrants lacking necessary skills, or the victims of natural calamities. Finally, there are neglected groups which while not actively exploited are less able to compete. Examples are the handicapped or aged. Together these segments may constitute a substantial underclass — perhaps as much as a fifth of the population. Although I do not insist on the precise proportion, I do assert that the proportion cannot be much larger on the assumption that the society has enjoyed liberal democratic institutions for a substantial period of time and has not suffered from war or natural calamity. The reason is that such institutions cannot survive unless a large segment of the population sees themselves as living in at least tolerable circumstances. Moreover, those institutions would tend to deliver to the remaining 80 percent at least some acceptable package of benefits and long-run expectations for the same reason. To fail to do so would create political opportunities which would, in the long run I have posited, certainly have been exploited.

The point of this hypothesis is that it permits a criterion by which to determine the level of the social minimum. Take the educational opportunities, health benefits, housing standards enjoyed by unionized unskilled workers, which I shall call the reference group. I choose this category since, as they are lacking skills, they are unlikely to be in a strong position to demand a market rent, but being unionized they will be able to assure themselves against systematic exploitation and will have an organizational structure sufficient to define long-term goals and to discipline its membership to persevere in their pursuit. The social minimum is whatever package of essential opportunities, goods, and services (as I shall explain the term *essential*) is enjoyed by the reference group. Note that this does not state that the social minimum is whatever *income* is enjoyed by this reference group, since presumably most members of that group will have further income and engage in further consumption of goods and services not deemed essential.

This standard is lower than the *average* consumption of those essential goods for two reasons: (1) To allow substantial play for the differentiating effects of individual choice and market forces, that is to avoid the kind of constant interference, regimentation, and aggressive leveling down that a more exigent standard of need would entail. (2) To recognize the fact that in respect to most of these goods there is a discretionary or non-essential component which is hard to separate out. This last is most obvious in respect to such goods as housing and diet, but applies as well to education, health, and perhaps legal services. In any event in the case of the United States the implementation of this standard would have a significant effect on the welfare of the most disadvantaged groups.

5. The reference group's consumption of essential goods is a function of the distribution of wealth in the particular society. If I am right, liberal democratic institutions will guarantee a certain substantial share to a group defined as I have. It may be objected that these reference levels change as the society changes, so that what constitutes justice at one time would be deemed unjust at another. If we had cut into the process in 1931 to make all the adjustments needed to insure a social minimum — as we probably did not — then the subsequent history of the system would have been different and so the adjustments required by the general criterion would be different in 1981 from what they are now in the absence of such earlier adjustments. In fact the objection might be pushed further. Since liberal democratic societies emerged from illiberal and unjust ones, often by at least partially evolutionary processes rather than by the sharp break of a total revolution, the citizens embark upon liberal democracy freighted with tastes and preferences found in an earlier distributionally *and* politically unhallowed past. Thus even if my distributional criterion were enacted at once as a part of the institution of democracy, still both the initial distribution and all its successors would seem to be tainted. There seems to be a kind of original sin which stains all subsequent attempts at virtue.

I believe this objection is irrelevant.[8] All I must show is that if the demands of distributive justice — the social minimum — had been implemented at some time in the past, say fifty or seventy-five years ago, what the social minimum requires today

---

[8] For valuable general arguments for the proposition that an ancient wrong, if not persisted in or renewed, has a relatively short half-life, see Nozick, *supra*, note 2, at 152–53; Scher, "Ancient Wrongs and Modern Rights," 19 *Philosophy and Public Affairs* 3 (1981).

would not be so different that my criterion for the social minimum must fall as circular. I concede right off that had a social minimum been instituted earlier many people would have been spared deprivations along the way. My argument is for a standard of just distribution *now*. It does not pretend that there have not been in the past and are not now unjust deprivations. Nor is there any reason to believe that the lowest group systematically able today to plan and provide for its essential goods (the reference group) would today enjoy a higher level of essential goods had the economic groups *beneath* it been assured a long time ago of these same essential goods — i.e., had the social minimum been assured in prior generations. If, for instance, the tax burdens necessary to provide the social minimum for all at an earlier date had lowered the rate of capital investment and entrepreneurial initiative of higher income groups — a point I do not here argue — then it might be that the income and therefore the level of spending for essential goods by the reference group today might actually be lower in a society which had been juster earlier, and the social minimum accordingly *less* exigent.

6. There is another similar objection to my proposal, and in answering it I can point to a general theme in my defense of a conception of liberty: the extent to which the standards which specify that conception can be and have to be independent of history, of culture and of politics. Since liberty is an ideal which claims to judge history, culture, and politics, it would seem to be undermined by any dependence on them, and yet some dependence seems inevitable. I propose a definite but limited and determinate standard of distribution: definite, because indifference to others is an offense to moral humanity; limited, because liberty requires a determinate domain of self-determination, free of the claims of others. I propose to measure the claim to redistribution by the level of essential goods enjoyed by unskilled, unionized workers. But it is the case that the situation of the reference class at any particular time is in part the product of politics, including redis-

tributive politics: Is free medical care available; is there subsidized housing; what is the level of spending on public education? In an egalitarian social democracy the situation of the reference group may be different from what it would be in a country with a more laissez-faire temperament. Yet — and now the objection closes in — my proposal is supposed to judge, rectify, and limit policies of redistribution by reference to a standard which must now be conceded to depend on the very variable and controversial policies it seeks to judge. If politics have won the reference group a certain level of mandated benefits at the moment we cut into the process, why should that level be frozen thenceforward as the absolute measure and limit of what it is just to accomplish by politics? In short, the objection states that by seeking determinacy I have attained only arbitrariness.

The objection misses the point, first technically and second in its basic conception. Technically, it must be remembered that I call for a redistributive floor not in terms of the *total* income of the reference class, but only in terms of their enjoyment of essential goods. The group I have designated is unlikely in any developed economy to rest content with consumption merely of essentials. Some important part of the group's activism, therefore, would have been directed at raising its level of discretionary (non-essential) income. Given the group's numerical importance their concern with discretionary income must necessarily impose a discipline on the demands for provision of essential services. Any increase in the consumption of essential goods by so significant a group will necessarily withdraw a large quantum of resources from the discretionary realm, and it is implausible that such a large burden could be shifted entirely to other groups. Thus, though it must be conceded that the reference group's overall situation may vary considerably from time to time and from society to society, and that those variations will depend on politics, nevertheless this group's enjoyment of essential goods may be said to approximate what a particular society at a particular state of development and prosperity considers a decent minimum.

7. I turn to a subtler, more insidious objection. First, it asks where do I get my list of essential goods from anyway. Second, it argues that the conception of what things are worthwhile, not to say essential, and a fortiori the decision of how essential these things are, how much to spend on them is internal to a socio-economic system and therefore cannot provide a criterion for the justice of fundamental features of a social system. In a capitalist society, it is said for instance, a private space, a home, distinctive clothing, and other items of personal consumption loom far larger than they would in a more egalitarian, socialist society which would value more highly attainments and opportunities to contribute to the common good. That's the story at any rate. But why should we believe it?

Everything turns on the possibility of identifying the contents (rather than the level) of the social minimum with sufficient confidence that the designation of its contents would survive the kind of social transformation which might accompany the shift from a political democracy to a completely just society. The skepticism on this score is one of the more plausible applications of the Kuhnian argument that conceptual terms do not retain their meaning across basic theories. Though philosophers of science dispute the validity and even the coherence of Kuhn's claim,[9] it has greatly impressed amateurs in law and the social sciences. Here the skeptical objection is clear enough: what constitutes a basic or essential or primary good is so obviously a cultural artifact that it cannot provide a criterion for judging alternative social arrangements.

The essential goods may be thought to be the same as the primary goods, which Rawls defines as those things a man would

---

[9] See, e.g., Hilary Putnam, *Mathematics, Matter and Method — Philosophical Papers*, vol. 1, 260 (Cambridge, 1975); Israel Scheffler, *Science and Subjectivity* (Indianapolis, 1967); Shapere " 'The Structure of Scientific Resolution,' " 73 *Phil. Rev.* 383 (1964).

want whatever else he wants: rights and liberties, powers and opportunities, income and wealth.[10] If income and wealth are defined in terms of money alone, the socially dependent nature of the price system which gives wealth its value shows that it is necessary to be more concrete than he has been about the components of wealth.[11] But I need only assume open democratic institutions and ask what material goods constitute a social minimum in such a society. The argument for the actual goods is then easy enough. I take education first.

Education is necessary to allow the members of the reference class to understand the functioning of the political system they participate in as citizens. Further, they must be able to obtain so much training as will enable them to take advantage of and compete for the opportunities available in an open economic system insofar as their natural abilities permit. And I suppose the entitlement extends to such education as will enable a person to participate in the culture of his society as well. The conditions of established democracy and of the political and economic awareness of the reference class explain the importance of this component of the social minimum: Education is just a precondition for intelligent choice, judgment about one's circumstances — including the choice about whether to include further education in one's vision of the good life. After all, the point of identifying the social minimum is to set the stage for individual free and fair choice. Health, housing, diet are only somewhat more problematical since their lack does not vitiate so definitively the idea of rational choice. Yet we must add them to the list. First, because rational choice is the rational choice of concrete human beings who require these things for the good functioning of their rational capacities. Second, because we are seeking to establish a reasonable measure for a

---

[10] *Supra*, note 2, at 62.

[11] See, e.g., Kennedy, "Cost Benefit Analysis of Entitlement Problems: A Critique," 33 *Stanford L. Rev.* 387, 422–23 (1981).

fair share of scarce resources, and those things necessary to sustain life and vigorous function are an obvious minimum in any system which recognizes need and community as aspects of a fair share.

Now all this is vague enough, but not fatally so, and certainly does not fall under the strictures of Kuhnian solipsism. Further, it is quite immune to the issue of the potentially voracious claims of handicapped persons who can only approach these educational or other standards by dint of enormous expenditures. I do not say they do not present a problem, but they do not present one for *this* theory. The criterion is constructed by reference to the natural capacities of the average member of the reference group. That there are those who require more attention is not a problem of distributive justice between income groups. It is, as it were, a random chance which affects citizens or families of *all* income classes.

8. It is natural to ask whether those entitled to benefits under the provision for the social minimum might be entitled instead to claim the cash value of those benefits, spending that cash on whatever they want. Economic theory teaches that cash payments are superior to in-kind distributions, since they (by hypothesis) cost the donor no more while leaving the beneficiary with enlarged options. This theorem fails to hold only if we posit some kind of market failure, on which I do not rely, or if we adopt toward the beneficiaries a paternalistic attitude, which I find distasteful. Yet I do conclude that there is an entitlement only to the essential goods themselves, not their cash equivalent. (I leave open — indeed I prefer — the possibility of giving a kind of restricted cash to beneficiaries, which can be used to purchase, say, health care on the market.) The reason derives from the basis of the entitlement: a particular kind of human need (misery), which we are morally bound not to ignore. It is the fact, for instance, that another person is, say, suffering from appendicitis which could be cured by hospitalization but which if uncured would lead to a painful death, it is that fact and not the fact that this same person

is so poor that he can't pay for the hospitalization which makes the claim upon us. If we imagine that we do give this person the money for an operation and he gives it to his lover to spend on liquor, the claim on us for help would still be there — we would not (and should not) allow him to die of a ruptured appendix and peritonitis. But this means that it *is* the medical care to which he is entitled and not anything else. I suppose he can decline to accept medical care; to force that on him would be paternalistic indeed. He has no right, however, to dictate the terms of the provision: if he does not wish medical care at all (or housing, or food, or other essential goods) then he just waives his claim on us altogether. This is not to say that under certain circumstances it may not be more practical and effective to give poor people, or certain classes of poor people, cash instead of goods or restricted money. That will depend on details of administration and politics. The principle, however, should be clear.

9. This brings me to the final question for this part and the bridge to the next: how important is it to a defense of liberty or to normative political philosophy generally that its points of reference themselves be fixed and neutral? My standard for a decent minimum seems to be neither. It is all mixed up with the changing political and economic arrangements of the subject society, and so seems ineligible as a standard to judge those arrangements. But it is a serious mistake to be disturbed by this. By demanding an impossible level of objectivity or neutrality such solidity as one is capable of is ignored or devalued. After all, the aim is to give meaning to the idea of a decent minimum so that it can stand as the compromise between our *right* to what we are and what we make and our *duty* to respond to the need and humanity of others. What is fixed, independent of, and can judge particular politics is just the wish to find such a compromise. So also the concept of a decent minimum as the further specification of that compromise is a concept independent of the particular politics it judges. The focus on a particular reference group in a democratic society and

on a particular part of that group's situation or budget makes the standard sufficiently independent of the politics it judges to provide discipline and control in that judgment. What we have is a changing standard, but one disciplined by a prescribed procedure (liberal democracy) and a prescribed concern (the identification of a decent minimum of essential goods). More than this, I think, it is unnecessary to ask, and at any rate I believe it is impossible to get.

PART II. MEANING AND CAUSE

1. A social minimum has been assured. There is fair opportunity for all and even those who fail, whose luck is bad, need not fear catastrophe. Given those conditions, liberty requires that we accept the outcome of individual transactions as not only efficient, but fair. If the choices made in the market are freely made, there is no sufficient reason to reverse or mitigate their effects, and whether those choices have been freely made is not a political, certainly not a distributive, judgment. (After all, the claims of distributive justice have been sufficiently met through the provision of the social minimum.) Rather it is a judgment of principle, legal principle, principle about such things as when an assurance makes a binding contract, the obligation of good faith in carrying out a contractual arrangement, when a person is liable to compensate for harm which he has caused but did not intend, whether a harm which would have befallen anyway is caused by an agent just because the agency would have been sufficient to cause the harm in other circumstances, whether someone who in good faith receives and spends money given him by mistake is bound to return it.

It is a tenet of liberalism shared by Ronald Dworkin[12] and positivists like H. L. A. Hart[13] that legal disputes between citizens

[12] *Taking Rights Seriously*, ch. 4 (Cambridge, Mass., 1978 ed.).
[13] *The Concept of Law*, chs. 5, 7 (Oxford, 1961).

are at least in large part decided as a matter of right. The parties are entitled to a decision by virtue of the preexisting law which it is the duty of the judge to apply. The differences between Dworkin and the positivists break out only in what Dworkin calls hard cases and in what Hart calls the penumbra of settled rules, where discretion is required. Dworkin carries the duty of judges to decide disputes according to law all the way through, so that even in hard cases (in which the positivists concede to the judge the role of policy-maker) the judge must apply principles rather than make policy furthering the collective goals of the community as a whole. Judgment, balance, principle are applicable in all cases — even those where the positivists claim a role for policy-making discretion. For Dworkin this exercise of judgment is the search for answers truly inhering in the legal and moral materials, principles the judge is bound to apply. It is crucial that this concept of law hold — either in its positivist or in its (to my mind richer and more coherent) Dworkinian version — if men are to be free, if liberty is to be possible. If judges were not (at least in large part) constrained by the law then the distinction between the right and the good would be gone, and all men would be servants of some authoritative view of collective policies and goals.

A liberal theory of law must accomplish at least these things:

A. It must allow persons to make agreements and it must enforce those agreements when made.

B. It must establish the boundaries around a person and his property so that incursions across those boundaries constitute compensable wrong.[14]

Tort law defines our rights. It draws the boundaries of what Hayek calls our private sphere,[15] within which we make the life we choose. The social minimum assures both that this private

---

[14] Cf. David Hume, *A Treatise of Human Nature* 526 (Selby-Bigge ed., Oxford, 1888).

[15] Friedrich Hayek, *The Constitution of Liberty* 21 (Chicago, 1960).

sphere will have certain minimum dimensions and that contributions to assure that minimum for others are themselves limited and fairly exacted. The notion of a private sphere is precisely correlated with the main aspects of liberty I set out in Part I: an individual's opportunity to choose her own life according to her own judgment, and responsibility for the consequences of her choices. If the boundaries of that sphere are fixed by the judgment of others about what are good outcomes of personal choices, then the individual is deprived of responsibility for her choices and thus of liberty of choice. She does not choose and act on her conception of the good; it is chosen for her. By contrast, when natural forces impinge on an individual's projects this does not derogate from her moral authority to determine those projects. It is only when the judgments of others impinge that liberty is at stake. Yet how can these boundaries be drawn other than as a result of a collective judgment? And, as we shall see, even so neutral-seeming a concept as cause, which may seem a natural candidate for identifying when another's conduct impinges on me or mine, is freighted with normative content.

Contract law is another indispensable aspect of liberty. The worth of my liberty is critically diminished if I cannot treat across my boundary with willing others. One of the things which I certainly want to do with what is assured to my discretion is to give it to others or trade it. When others impede my gifts or exchanges they assert an authority not just over me but over my partner as well, an authority therefore doubly offensive to liberty. And promises are simply gifts or exchanges projected into the future. By recognizing and enforcing promises society enlarges liberty.[16] By selectively refusing to enforce some promises because of how the promisors use their liberty, or because of who ends up better off because of them, or who the promisor is, the collectivity is again

[16] See Immanuel Kant, *The Metaphysical Elements of Justice*, Ladd trans., 54–55 [248] (Indianapolis, 1965).

asserting an authority over individuals which is incompatible with their liberty. Of course only those obligations freely contracted warrant this recognition. Yet the notion of what is freely undertaken, and how the content of those undertakings can be understood, is controversial. What is fraud, what duress — these are normative questions. So also may be the fixing of the meaning of general terms.

Liberty requires conceptions of private law based on principles, not on episodic collective judgments of policy. But given these controversies about tort and contract, are such conceptions available?

2. Contract requires a theory of language which assumes the stable and common identification of the subject matter of commitment. Given the controversies about the indeterminacy of translation, we see that even about present exchanges there may be problems.[17] But how much worse are the problems for promising, which makes commitments into the future and thus requires a theory of the identity of singular objects over time in addition to a theory of the identity of reference by two persons referring simultaneously. There is the famous case of Rose II of Aberlone, the prize breeding cow sold off at the price of beef because her owner thought her sterile, while in fact she was not only fertile but pregnant and worth a hundred times that price.[18] Or the case of the mysterious stone sold for a dollar which turned out to be an uncut diamond.[19] Or the rooms rented for a day at fancy prices to view a coronation procession which never took place.[20] Much ink has been spilled applying theories about the identity of objects to such cases and debating whether changed attributes imply a change

---

[17] Cf. W. V. Quine, *Word and Object*, ch. 2 (Cambridge, Mass., 1960).

[18] Sherwood v. Walker, 66 Mich. 568, 33 N.W. 919 (1887).

[19] Wood v. Boynton, 64 Wis. 265, 25 N.W. 42 (1885).

[20] Griffith v. Brymer, 19 T. L. R. 434 (K. B. 1903); Krell v. Henry, 2 K. B. 740 (1903).

in subject matter.[21] These cases have engendered metaphysical speculation which would delight Saul Kripke[22] and Hilary Putnam:[23] Does not Rose II of Aberlone designate a particular cow irrespective of mistaken attributes?

Even such problems as that may be dismissed as of no practical significance. What cannot be so easily dismissed, however, is the problem of general terms. Both H. L. A. Hart[24] and John Austin before him[25] noted that law — by practical necessity — must use general terms lest it be relegated to a system of simple singular commands. The same is, of course, true of promises. To accomplish regimes of coordination and cooperation of any complexity, promises/contracts must be cast in general terms as well. And that's where the difficulties begin. They break out in problems of interpretation, of course, but most obviously in the cases collected under the rubrics of mistake, impossibility, and frustration.

Whether this issue is one of the designation of singular terms or the meaning of general terms, for the purposes of contract law the question should be: had the parties come to an actual agreement about the relevant risks such that the promise principle is properly invoked? And this is a question at least in principle susceptible of an answer. The appropriate inquiry must relate to the intentions of the parties rather than the canons of fairness that take over when it appears that the parties had no convergent intention in the premises. Agreement — convergent substantive intentions (about risks and values of stones and cows) embodied in

21 For reviews of the literature, see Bronaugh, "The Place of Identity in Contract Formation," 18 *U. W. Ontario L. Rev.* 185 (1980); Francis de Zulueta, *The Roman Law of Sale: Introduction and Select Texts* 28–30 (Oxford, 1945).

22 Saul Kripke, *Naming and Necessity* (Cambridge, Mass., 1980); "Identity and Necessity" in Stephen Schwartz, ed., *Naming, Necessity and Natural Kinds* (Ithaca, N.Y., 1977).

23 "Meaning and Reference," in Schwartz, *supra*.

24 *Supra*, note 13, at 21.

25 *The Province of Jurisprudence Determined*, Lecture I (H. L. A. Hart ed., London, 1954).

the intentional invocation of the promissory form — is one category, and fairness in picking up the pieces after it becomes evident
that the parties had sailed out together in a leaky boat (a defective
agreement) quite another. I make this distinction for the sake of
liberty. If the law's, the courts' substantive grounds of fairness
threaten to come in each time to tell *what* the agreement is, then
it is the judges who make the contract and not the parties.

3. There is an argument for the proposition that the courts do
in fact and inevitably make contracts for the parties which has
gained currency among some legal writers. The argument takes
as its point of departure the philosophical problem about general
terms. General terms, as the argument goes, are attempts to sweep
a large set of particulars under a single conceptual rug; but it is an
attempt doomed to failure. General terms have no objective corre-
lates; they are merely compendia of particulars collected together
for our convenience in terms of similarities we note for our purposes. To say that general terms have no objective reality is to say
first that general terms do not of themselves identify the particulars subsumed under them, and *second* that therefore the process
of subsumption is a value-laden process, one which refers to
human goals and purposes. Since agreements which work into
the future are cast by a practical necessity in general terms, then
the process of interpreting the agreement is a value-laden process,
not an impartial search for the intention of the parties.[26] And
therefore the courts cannot escape making contracts for the parties
and liberty is *pro tanto* impossible. This argument might be refined
somewhat — perhaps along these lines: Fried says that a contract
is really about a set of risks — about the value of a stone, a cow,
or a view from a window. And, the argument continues, as soon as
the dispute relates to matters which have not just precisely and

---

[26] See Grant Gilmore, *The Death of Contract* (Columbus, Ohio, 1974); Morton
Horwitz, *The Transformation of American Law*, 184–85 (Cambridge, Mass., 1966);
Kennedy, "Form and Substance in Private Law Adjudication," 89 *Harv. L. Rev.* 1685
(1965).

explicitly been included in that set, as soon as one must extrapolate, as soon as one must ask the meaning or the intention of that set, one has been cut loose from the solid shore of the parties' intention and is adrift on a sea of indeterminacy.[27] And in that case the court may as well impose its values, since someone must.

Exactly the same point comes up in the case of good faith. In the recent case of *Fortune* v. *National Cash Register*,[28] Fortune had for over twenty years worked for NCR under a contract allowing him to quit on sixty days' notice and to be fired on ninety days' notice. His employer exercised this option shortly after Fortune procured a five-million-dollar order for NCR, an order which would have required the payment of large bonuses to Fortune over several years if he had been kept on. The court balked at this bad faith on the employer's part. The skeptical objection to the liberal conception of contract would say that here plainly the parties had not thought of just this eventuality. Nor will the objection allow the court's solution to be described as the determination of the extension of the general conception of the arrangement by an intuition of its intention, i.e., its meaning, as one might say that a man who used the term "all the primes between 0 and 1000" meant to include 719 though that number had not entered his head. Not a bit of it — the critic insists that the court is simply imposing its conception of fairness on the parties.

Now one will recognize here analogues to Wittgenstein's discussion of "continuing the series." [29] It is that discussion which sinks this skeptical argument. For we have learned that an account of our capacity to understand general terms, to follow rules, is not like the description of a train moving along tracks — there is not some necessity wholly apart from our purposes, apart from the

---

[27] Cf. Kennedy, "Legal Formality," 2 *J. Legal Studies* 351 (1973).

[28] 373 Mass. 96, 364 N. E. 2d 1251 (1977).

[29] *Philosophical Investigations*, §§136–242 (Anscombe trans., Oxford, 1953). See also Crispin Wright, *Wittgenstein on the Foundations of Mathematics*, ch. 2 (Cambridge, Mass., 1980).

way we are which draws us on. The referents of general terms
are not objectively, metaphysically real (to use Hilary Putnam's
term)[30] in that sense. Indeed, once we confront the idea squarely
one doesn't even know what that kind of objectivity would look
like if it were the correct description. Yet rules and the referents
of general terms are quite objective enough — they are (to para-
phrase Putnam again) internally real. They are real — they draw
us on — *inside* the world of purposes and experiences we inhabit,
the only world we know. The skeptical critic may pounce on this
as proving his supposed point — for how, he will ask, can we be
sure we inhabit the same worlds: promisors, promisees and judges?
But it is too obvious that if we did not inhabit the same world
communication would be impossible, including the communication of the skeptic's proposals and refutations. To be sure, we do
not have the same purposes: trivially, because my purposes are
always mine and so at best our purposes run parallel to each other;
more substantively, because our purposes often pull in quite different directions. But there is no more problem due to this than
there is due to the evident fact that our perceptions also — trivially
and substantively — are not the same. Our successful communica-
tions show that we share purposes and perceptions to a sufficient
degree. That they also diverge gives us something to talk about.

   One might ask how the judge at one and the same time can
share the values and perspective of the contracting parties so that
she is able to interpret their will and yet stand ready to disagree
with what the parties have accomplished, so that she leaves them
enough space to do what they want, not what she wants. The
answer that common experience proposes distinguishes between
that sharing of goals which is necessary to make general terms
commonly comprehensible and the closer sharing which comes
when we are in agreement on particular goals. Wittgenstein's

---

[30] *Reason, Truth and History* (Cambridge, England, 1981); "Realism and Reason," in *Meaning and the Moral Sciences* (London, 1978).

talk of "forms of life" and Putnam's insistence that general terms — natural kinds — are relative to our needs and ends[31] all point to this same phenomenon which common sense too identifies: To understand each other we must at least be able to imagine what it would be like to have the other person's goals. And the practice of sociology, anthropology, philology, far from supporting the crude skepticism of the cultural relativist is wholly encouraging on this score, as it shows how far we can indeed go in making transparent what seemed opaque. The possibilities of understanding demonstrated by these disciplines — as by the evident fact of the translatability of languages quite remote from our own in time and cultural distance — are remarkable.

It makes sense, I think, to speak of our common humanity as largely coextensive with the kind of shared form of life necessary to attain understanding. This is not to say that we always understand each other at once and without a sometimes considerable imaginative effort. And of course we run the risk that we not only will understand initially alien conceptions but come to share them. Similarly our understanding of another person's goals may convince us that we have a better grasp of some of the entailments of those goals than their original proponent. This is the kernel of truth in the objections we have been considering. This is the idea which Fuller captured in the phrase that the common law works itself pure.[32] But it is pure sophistry to conclude from this that therefore it is the judge's goals which every time control after all, when it is the task of a judge to determine what the goals and commitments of others may have been. And it is a further kernel of truth that contracting parties (or any users of general language) often seek to enlist the cooperation of a third party in drawing out the entailments of their own arrangements. In such cases they may also want the third party to use his own particular ends and values in performing

---

31 *Supra*, notes 23 and 30.
32 Lon L. Fuller, *The Law in Quest of Itself* (Chicago, 1940).

this operation. All this is true, but it still does not lead to the conclusion that there is not a distinct operation in which it is the other
person's goals we are trying to understand. And so as to understanding and interpretation, we might say that the shared goals —
way of life — are the ground which makes diverse goals perspicuous to us.

And so the doubt that promisors, promisees, and judges can
determine general intentions which are transparent all around is
just another case of sophomoric general skepticism, and not worth
agonizing over. It is worth seeing that the form of this answer to
the skeptical objection is related to what I argued earlier about the
standard of distributive justice. There too we seemed to be stymied
by the demand for a wholly objective measure of fair shares, until
we saw that a standard could be defined as what emerged from the
common experience of democratic institutions, and moreover that
it was perfectly all right for that standard to change, that such
changeability did not imply a fatal subjectivity in the standard.
The standpoint of internal realism (as opposed to metaphysical
realism), realistic though it is, does not promise immobility, a
fixed right answer, from the perspective of some universal and
uninvolved observer. And yet to the involved observer every
difference of judgment is the occasion for argument in which each
participant acknowledges the possibility of his or his interlocuter's
(or both) transcending a particular point of view and coming to
a new truth.

4. A theory of gifts and exchanges is useless, however, without a theory of what is ours to give, what are our interests and
against what they are protected. We need a theory of tort law.
Two recent authors greatly concerned with liberty, Robert Nozick
and Richard Epstein, see the matter this way: There is a system of
property rights, including of course rights in the integrity of our
own physical person. Anyone who impinges on those rights is
prima facie liable to compensate the aggrieved party. Nozick char-

acterizes the impingements as boundary crossings.[33] For Epstein the prima facie rule is one of strict liability: If you cause harm to another's protected interest, you must pay.[34] Thus the topological paradigm of a personal boundary to be secured against all incursions is carried forward. But of course the concept of cause must now bear a heavy burden in the account. If a man stores a dangerous substance on his land and it escapes without his further intervention is he or is he not the cause of the harm?[35] Is a person who remains or allows his property to remain in the way of a potentially damaging force a contributing cause? Epstein speaks of a person as being a cause when he releases a force which brings about the harm, or when he stores up a force which brings about the harm as a consequence of the application of some slight additional force.[36] And, following Hart and Honore,[37] he holds further that something is a cause when it is one of a jointly sufficient set of conditions for that result, and the result comes about without the intervention either of a voluntary human agency or some unusual circumstance.[38] This conception of cause they claim is embedded in both ordinary usage and the common law.

One sees why Epstein puts it this way. The picture is of a status quo, a base line which the actor disturbs. Behind his idea is Nozick's, Kant's, Locke's conception of a private domain which defines the individual's discretionary space, within which he can work out his conception of happiness. It is the state's, the law's, duty to protect this privacy. Epstein's conception of causality hopes to permit the simplest possible conception of boundary

---

[33] *Supra*, note 2, at 57.

[34] The corpus of Epstein's writing is large. His views are summarized in a recent essay, "Nuisance Law: Corrective Justice and Its Utilitarian Constraints" (hereafter "Nuisance Law"), 8 *J. Legal Studies* 49 (1979). The primary article is "A Theory of Strict Liability," 2 *J. Legal Studies* 151 (1973).

[35] Epstein, "Nuisance Law," *supra*, at 66–68.

[36] "A Theory of Strict Liability," *supra*, note 34, at 166–68, 177–78.

[37] H. L. A. Hart and A. M. Honore, *Causation in the Law* (Oxford, 1959).

[38] "Nuisance Law," *supra*, note 34, at 56–60; "A Theory of Strict Liability," *supra*, note 34, at 160–89.

crossing, and thus to implicate the sparest possible system of judgments in determining whether rights have been infringed. If they have been, then compensation is due. In other words, compensation is not compelled, rights protected for forward-looking reasons of the community, but rather just in recognition of those rights. This is what is classically called corrective justice,[39] contrasted to distributive justice or to the pursuit of other policy goals of the community.

Thus the causal theory may be seen as seeking to do for tort law what I have tried to do for contract law — which is to show how legal rules and institutions do (or with some changes, can be made to) recognize individual rights by carrying out the determination of private wills. Epstein's picture, which I linger over because it is so intuitively powerful, is intended to assure that tort law is moved not by considerations of economic efficiency, or distributive concerns, or any policy, but just by a concern to vindicate the rights of the parties to the dispute. Strict liability plus causality appear to do just that. Did the defendant's act invade the plaintiff's right? If it did, the associated harm must be compensated.

5. Unfortunately, causation is a normative, not to say a controversial, concept. Hart and Honore's proposal, for instance, depends on the absence of "unusual" intervening events. And that is a matter of evaluation. For Epstein the case is much worse, since for him (though not for Hart and Honore) causing harm is prima facie tortious. Would anything a man does which enters into a set of conditions sufficient to bring about the harm be culpable? Would planting a tree on your lawn which twenty years later is blown onto a passing car be culpable? Not so, Epstein would respond: a cause, as opposed to a condition, is active; it is the application of force, or the storing of force easily released. If defendant has walked across plaintiff's land trampling his flower

---

[39] See Aristotle, *Nicomachean Ethics*, Bk. V, iv–v; Epstein, "Nuisance Law," *supra*, at 50. For a different view, see Richard Posner, *The Economics of Justice*, at 73–74 (Cambridge, Mass., 1951).

garden, the causal paradigm seems unproblematic, but if that is the easy case, hard cases unfortunately are the rule.

First, every case with a moving plaintiff and a moving defendant (the typical road accident which makes up the vast bulk of tort cases) involves *mutual* impingement.

Second, it runs counter to at least 150 years of law to make the question of liability depend on whether the defendant was moving and the plaintiff still regardless whether the defendant made reasonable efforts to consider the plaintiff's interest.[40] Imagine the case of the careful motorist who injures plaintiff pedestrian as the result of a skid on an unnoticeable patch of ice.

Third, every effect is the resultant not of some single, isolatable factor but of an infinite manifold of circumstances, which is only carved down into discrete conceptual packets for an explanatory purpose. In the case of the skidding motorist one description of the event might focus on the force originating in the kinetic energy of the automobile's engine. And to push inquiry back beyond this to the action of the motorist in turning the ignition key but not further still to the conduct of those who assembled the car or refined the gasoline is a selective judgment based on our explanatory or other social purpose.[41] Similarly, the focus on forces is at times inappropriate. If the icy patch had been intentionally or negligently placed in the roadway, or (to modify an example of Epstein's) if a defendant walking along an unlit corridor steps on a roller skate left there and blunders into plaintiff, whose arm he breaks, the force is all the defendant's, but the cause and blame is his who created the dangerous condition. Epstein holds a man to be *the* cause of harm if he stores up potential energy in such a way that a small extraneous force will cause its harmful release. And so it is with conditions generally. The presence of oxygen in the air is not *the* cause of a fire set in the

---

[40] See, e.g., Brown v. Kendall, 60 Mass. (6 Cush.) 291 (1850).
[41] Hart and Honore, *supra*, note 37, at ch. 2.

open by defendant which spreads to plaintiff's property. Neither
is a light breeze which comes up after the fire is started. If, however, an unusual wind spreads the fire to plaintiff's property, or
oxygen is introduced into a chemical reaction begun by defendant
which in the absence of oxygen would have progressed slowly and
with no harm to anyone, then these intervening events may well
usurp the sobriquet of cause.[42]

Fourth, at the other end of the physical process, what counts
as harm is hardly a matter to be settled on purely physical or
topological grounds: whether a force was imparted across a
designated line.

Epstein sees heat, sound, concussion waves from explosions,
odors and gases as instances of invading objects or transmitted
energy.[43] Here his physics is beyond reproach but misses the point
that light may come in the form of a destructive laser beam or as
a spotlight on an outdoor movie screen[44] or as the dim but deci-
pherable bearer of an offensive image. Sound may be shattering,
or merely discordant, or the bearer of a disturbing message.
Whether or not the intrusion is harmful will be a function of
factors other than the physical magnitude of the force. Thus,
for instance, a modicum of noise or light introduced onto another's
property will not be actionable, but the very idea that the house
next to mine is being used as a funeral parlor might be. (Epstein
says that the funeral parlor-as-nuisance cases are wrong because
ideas are not physical forces.[45] But images are, and they carry the
idea which turns out to be noxious. A discordant noise becomes
noxious because of its form, not because of its acoustical pressure,
yet here Epstein does see a possible nuisance.) Indeed it is not
clear why only positive intrusions should be actionable. Corre-

---

[42] See, Hart and Honore, at 31–38.

[43] "Nuisance Law," *supra*, note 34, at 60.

[44] See Amphitheaters, Inc. v. Portland Meadows, 184 Ore. 336, 198 P.2d 847
(1948).

[45] "Nuisance Law," *supra*, note 34, at 64–65.

sponding to the light shone upon your movie screen would be the erection of a barrier blocking the sun from your bathing beach[46] or greenhouse. Corresponding to the offensive images projected onto your property would be the erection of a barrier to a delightful view. Is it crucial whether you project a light or a shadow — or a combination of light and shadow forming an image? It should be said that Epstein resolutely hews to his physicalist line, finding the light actionable but not the shadow.[47]

Nor can one escape these difficulties by a more careful definition of the rights, the boundaries, in issue: Is there a right to "ancient lights," to a view, to quiet? If so, then to interfere with that is tortious. We are then driven to ask why are these conceptual boundaries not normatively permeable to some but not to other forces — permeability being a function of probability of risk, motive, type of force. Perhaps, for instance, noise only crosses my boundary at nighttime, because the boundary, like Goodman's grue emeralds, is defined in spatio-temporal terms. Or consider the right to one's good name or to a purely residential neighborhood — free of funeral homes as neighbors. These considerations show that neither the concept of cause nor that of a spatial boundary which a defendant causes a force to transgress are as normatively neutral or even as coherent as one would wish for the purposes of a tort system which respects individual liberty.

6. The difficulties in Epstein's conception of cause can be traced to his treatment of cause as an exclusively physical relation between events: the impact of a brick causing a window to shatter. As Mill pointed out, however, there is an infinity of conditions — negative and positive — which must concur for a given effect to obtain.[48] Which of these is designated *the* cause seems not to be determined by something about the conditions themselves, nor yet

---

[46] See, Fountainbleau Hotel Corp. v. Forty-Five–Twenty-Five, Inc., 114 So. 2d 35 (1959).

[47] "Nuisance Law," *supra*, note 34, at 61–62.

[48] For a discussion of Mill's views, see Hart and Honore, *supra*, note 36, at 12–21.

by the kind of physical relation in which a condition stands to the effect. Rather it is an explanatory relation. To use an example from Hart and Honore, different people may consider the speed of the train, the degree of the grade, or the displacement of a slightly bent rail as the cause of the train wreck, depending on their explanatory purposes.[49] But explanation is not a physical relation.

On the other hand there is more reason to go along with the common-sense view that cause is a singular relation.[50] Although scientific laws and regularities may stand behind the singular event (brick shattering window) we do not need to know them to know the cause. "Why did the window break?" "Because Johnny threw a brick through it." This is a perfectly satisfactory explanation. Accounts in terms of the strength of the molecular bonds in glasses may be a further explanation, or an explanation of the explanation, but contrary to the covering law hypothesis[51] it is not at all clear why we must have such further explanations before we are warranted in making the judgment that the brick shattered the glass.[52] One may venture the guess that it is this sense of cause being a singular relation that leads ordinary persons to think of it also as an exclusively physical relation. You feel it in your bones when the force of your body causes something to move, break, collapse. The very causal vocabulary is singular: cut, smash, break, slash, pierce, kill.

But why do we pass from the singularity of the causal relation to the conclusion that it is an exclusively physical, metaphysically real relation?" Because of our pervasive tendency to project our purposes and interests on the world in which we play them out. If you accept the conception of cause as explanation relative to a purpose or interest, and if certain purposes and interests are

[49] *Supra*, note 41.

[50] See, generally, G. E. M. Anscombe, *Causality and Determination* (Cambridge, 1971); Davidson, "Causal Relations," 64 *J. Phil.* 691 (1967).

[51] Carl Hempel, "Aspects of Scientific Explanation," in *Aspects of Scientific Explanation and Other Essays in the Philosophy of Science* (New York, 1965).

[52] See Anscombe, *supra*, note 50.

pervasive, constant, deep-rooted, such a projection of a singular relation on the outside world is altogether natural. It does not even seem wholly mistaken since after all we construct the world out of our experiences and interests. Causes are natural as kinds are natural — i.e., relative to the way we are in the world.[53]

We may, then, make an argument about causing boundary crossings analogous to the argument about the use of general terms to embody agreements. And thus we would put tort law on as secure a footing as contract law, and this part of the task of a theory of liberty would be accomplished. We must regretfully say goodbye to Epstein's account in terms of imparting force or releasing forces. His account does no more than substitute a more general causal account for the more familiar particular causal accounts of breaking, kicking, turning on or off, without any gain in clarity or insight. It is just plausible to say that, prima facie, we wrong another when we kick him, break his arm or burn down his house. It is palpably implausible to utter Epstein's generalization about the wrongness of doing harm by imparting or releasing forces. Either we stay at the level of concrete relations altogether or we move to quite a different set of categories.

7. As I have argued, Epstein's account is defective in part because it misses the need to identify the boundaries which must not be crossed, the interests which may not be impinged upon. The boundaries of one's personal space may be drawn variously and the lines need not be limited to the three dimensions — they may include time or risk and be permeable (ethically permeable) to some but not all intrusions. How are they to be drawn, then? An a priori answer seems beyond our grasp. Yet if the boundaries are drawn (as the law-and-economics, justice-as-efficiency analysis of tort law would have it) to accomplish extrinsic social ends,[54]

---

[53] Cf. Putnam, *Reason, Truth and History, supra,* note 30; R. G. Collingwood, "On the So-Called Idea of Causation," 38 *Proceedings of the Aristotelian Society* 85 (1938).

[54] See, Epstein, "A Theory of Strict Liability," *supra,* note 34, at 203–4; Charles Fried, *Right and Wrong,* ch. 4 (Cambridge, Mass., 1978).

then it is those ends and not the recognition of individual rights which stand behind the law of torts. Individual liberty is not secure if its contours depend on the convenience of others. Rights, it would then seem, are either natural, necessary, a priori, and so secure, and liberty secure with them, or *merely* conventional and our liberty at the mercy of collective judgments of policy. But this is just the same false dichotomy which we faced in respect to distribution and agreement. The boundaries of our persons and property cannot be anything other than conventional — in the sense that they are not given independently but are discerned in the context of human needs and concerns.

I propose that two sets of conventions (let us call them that for the moment) work together to identify wrongful invasions: conventions about what the boundaries are and conventions about when a boundary is wrongfully crossed. They work together, but they are not the same. (You could make them the same by defining the boundary and its permeability in highly abstract non-topological terms, so that for instance we might say that a non-negligent entry onto a topologically defined space or an accidental blow to my person doesn't cross the boundary of my normatively defined space while, say, a negligent intrusion or an intentional blow would.) I would not collapse the questions of boundary and of intrusion because our tort theory should capture the distinction between what's mine or what's me (boundaries) on one hand and what is a wrongful act on the other. Both are conventional. There is no natural way of dividing up moral space any more than there is of dividing up the objects in the world — yet the conventions go very deep. The boundaries of my physical person are as palpable and fundamental as the individuating segments of the manifold of experienced reality.[55] As to objects and land, however, the conventions are often no firmer than the set of things we need and value in our activities, and so those conventions change with our interests.

[55] Ibid., at ch. 2.

All this must be pinned down and illustrated with specifics. At this point I want to refer to the parallel to the other component, the causal component of tort theory. Causal terms — break, burn, shatter — also embody our interests. They do so by reflecting the ways in which we intervene in natural processes to effect those interests. Indeed the very phrase "intervene in natural processes to . . ." is a studied equivocation, for it seems virtually impossible to discuss the interplay between ourselves and the world without invoking such causal terms or their analogues. An account of the world just in terms of sequenced sets of conditions would be impenetrably opaque. It could accommodate neither moral advice nor moral judgment. So why should we flee the greater richness of our causal vocabulary? Because it lacks neutrality vis-à-vis our goals and interests? But there is no reason to yearn for that.

And this points the parallel between the active (causal) and passive (boundary) portions of the tort question. The drive for neutrality comes, I am sure, from the same drive as the drive to define a stable and uniform criterion of distributive justice, and at a more general level to profess a theory of language and of truth which is secure and valid from a point of view outside of the world we occupy. The concepts of cause are palpable and real enough; they are just not *metaphysically* real. The crucial question is not — it *never* is — whether the boundaries of me and mine, whether the concept of cause are real in this impossible sense, but rather whether such contingency as they inevitably have makes them useless to define rights and wrongs and thus useless to serve in establishing the concept of liberty. As to cause, the concepts are stable or common enough. We can understand each other's use of causal terms, just as we can understand each other's use of general terms; we can translate. Translation is possible because of a common human nature. That human nature is not some third, deeper common language we both share and into which we translate our different languages when we understand each other. Just as we do not translate to this ghostly common language when we

understand each others' same surface language. Surface languages
are all there are, and in understanding and translating we stay on
that surface. So it is with cause. We may disagree about, change,
or deepen our ideas about intervening in the world, about ourselves being active and producing results, but as we do, it is
not because we are getting deeper in touch with some underlying causal notion: producing changes in the world. "Producing
changes in the world" is a generalized causal notion which is only
as good as the ways in which we produce changes in the world —
by breaking, burning, pushing, ionizing, lasing — it is not itself
a way of producing changes in the world.

So if in tort law we are interested in rightful and wrongful
conduct, we are interested in rightful and wrongful ways in which
people produce changes in the world. The causal aspect, then, of
tort law is no simpler but no more complicated than that. Epstein's
mistake is to seek an explication of cause in terms of some deeper,
unified idea of producing changes in the world as such. And as
we saw, he came up with some rather bizarre but not always un-
illuminating notions about releasing stored forces and so on. If
you do things my way, then there is no reason to shrink from saying that the person who casts shadows is a causal agent every bit
as much as one who shines a light. Or that one who poisons a
reputation is a causal agent just as one who poisons a well. True,
our repertoire of causal notions will change as our repertoire of
causal means changes. If we cease to believe in witchcraft, putting
a hex on somebody ceases to be a way of effecting changes in the
world, but now altering their genetic structure may be. Though
there is change there is total translatability, which is all we need.
The causal concepts are quite universal: no one can hex or be
hexed, and anyone might change or be changed in respect to
genetic structure.

8. An analogous approach is in order when it comes to drawing the boundaries of our rights: the bounds within which I may
act even if I do harm you, and the bounds within which you are

secure from my incursions. Even the bounds of my person are conventional but relative to the most pervasive conceptions. More contingent is the question of negligent impingements on my person. How much attention do you have to pay to my potential presence in going about your projects? The answer there will be closely related not to the idea of the person, but to property. If I am driving along the highway then I am far more open to being hit by you as you drive on that highway (morally open, of course) than if I am rocking on my porch at home. We are both going about our business on common property, in a common area. To ask me to be too attentive to the risk of hitting you is to allow you to take over what is common property. We must divide it up: not just by drawing a line down the topological middle, but also by drawing a notional line down the middle of the risks we suffer and impose there. Not so on my front porch, perhaps. There I should be quite secure — and it is not too much of an inhibition to say that if you blunder on me there, you must pay for the harm you do.

And what then are the boundaries of my property? Those lines are highly conventional, in the sense that they are changed frequently and deliberately. I suspect that it is this variability above all which leads to the conclusion that tort law, and thus the extent of private rights, is a creature of and subject to public policy. Of course if that is true, then as to property the force does go out of the concept of liberty. Liberty is correlative to rights — my liberty is the discretion I enjoy within the notional sphere of my rights. As to the boundaries of my person the principles are general, pervasive. Though these principles develop and are influenced by the social systems and material circumstances which evolve against the background of these rights, I hope I have made it clear that this should not undermine these principles as principles, nor tempt us to try to step outside of our conceptual skins. Such arguments are, however, progressively less convincing as we move from personal to property rights and from property rights closely associated with personality (e.g., privacy of one's home or rights to choice of profession) to property rights involving large-scale economic enterprise. All I want to say about even the most extreme end of that spectrum is that there is a large difference between the community pursuing its policies (economic development, protection of the environment, national prestige or defense) by creating rights and by adopting a directly managerial role.[56] The regime of property rights represents a compromise between collective concerns (which determine the specific contours of property rights) and a respect for individuals, whose collaboration is enlisted on the understanding that they retain the measure of discretion that *any* right implies. Indeed, to withdraw all relations to things from the regime of rights would render largely nugatory the natural right to one's own person and efforts, for those efforts are expended on the outside world. Nor is the changeability of property rights an insurmountable obstacle, so long as changes are gradual or prospective. A sharp, retrospective change in definition does, however, amount to confiscation.

9. How do we establish where the boundaries fall, what is included within our conception of cause, what are the fair implications of general terms, what does fairness require when contractual arrangements fail? In general the method for specifying rights and wrongs is the method of reflective equilibrium.[57] At the specific level we may have to rely on the more intuitive method of argument by analogy. Analogistic reasoning, which is the staple of the law, is a poor cousin of reflective equilibrium. An analogy is an implicit invocation of an unstated principle, an inchoate theory, which it is believed or hoped will justify both the decision analogized from and the decision analogized to. Neither method pretends to deductive or a prioristic necessity; it is content to work with the convictions which develop within an existing situation,

[56] See Charles Fried, *Contract as Promise* 99–103 (Cambridge, Mass., 1981); Dworkin, *supra*, note 12, at 297–311.

[57] See John Rawls, *A Theory of Justice* §§1, 87.

conceding the necessity for their criticism and refinement, but never hoping in some way to step outside of the skin of the considered judgments of actual moral reasoners. It is my claim that citizens and judges working within a legal tradition are able to develop rules of property and tort law, rules about boundaries and causation, in this implicit way: that this development is sufficiently gradual and in sufficient touch with the common morality of the community that Dworkin's and Hayek's conception of the common law as (relatively) impersonal has sufficient validity.[58]

Both argument by analogy and Rawls's reflective equilibrium have come under attack. Reflective equilibrium, as is well known, depends on considered judgments. These considered judgments, it is objected, are merely subjective intuitions, personal preference.[59] The same criticism applied to argument by analogy urges that what will seem like a close or a distinct analogy is once again a mere matter of intuition at best, naked subjectivity at worst. A number of authors have converged on a somewhat half-hearted defense of rationality against these criticisms. The first was Edward Levi in his classic work, *An Introduction to Legal Reasoning.*[60] Levi was ready to concede (quite unnecessarily in my view) that argument by analogy is imperfect reasoning (at best it is a form of implicit inductive reasoning) and to concede as well that in the event it only gives form to the changing policy judgments of judges. The one saving feature which he found in common law argument from precedent, common law argument by analogy, is that it takes place in a public forum, with the affected parties urging their competing analogies, and the judge being compelled to offer a justification for the conclusion he finally announces on the basis of these analogies. That same idea is repeated and becomes

---

[58] Dworkin, *supra*, note 12; Hayek, *supra*, note 15, at Part II.

[59] See, Noble, "Normative Ethical Theories," 62 *Monist* 496, at note 5 (1979); Shaw, "Intuition and Moral Philosophy," 17 *Am. Phil. Q.* 127 (1980).

[60] Chicago, 1949, at 1–27.

central in Lon Fuller's posthumous work "The Forms and Limits of Adjudication" [61] and receives its most elegant form in a chapter of Ronald Dworkin's *Taking Rights Seriously* called "Justice and Rights." [62]

Dworkin, commenting directly on Rawls's method of reflective equilibrium, demurs to the proposition that this method will yield some kind of objective moral truth. The method has independent force and validity, in Dworkin's view, as a method of *public* controversy and *public* decision-making. The necessity for judges to consider competing arguments, to propose principles standing behind their judgments, to seek in their opinions to make these principles acceptable to the community and to relate this acceptability to a demonstration that the newly announced decision is part of the community's own moral sense and moral theory; this public posture, says Dworkin, gives the conclusions of judges a weight and a legitimacy, a title to the obedience and respect of the community, which is independent of any claims about the objective moral truth of the proposition announced. All three of these authors, Levi, Fuller, and Dworkin, thus make no claims for their preferred method (and mine) in terms of moral truth: their claims are rather to the reasonableness and legitimacy of the result so achieved.

Levi, Fuller, and Dworkin are quite correct in emphasizing the essentially public nature of moral argument and moral discourse. It would be a mistake, however, to conclude therefore that such public arguments are at best *only* legitimate, that they do not merit the sobriquet of validity or truth. This conclusion would be a mistake because it supposes that moral argument can ever be anything other than in principle public. To be sure, you or I may carry on an intense moral inquiry in total, silent privacy, preparatory to making some deep and important decision. It is a mistake

[61] 92 *Harv. L. Rev.* 353 (1978).

[62] *Supra*, note 12, at ch. 6.

to imagine that this process represents the true form of moral deliberation, and argument before a court, for instance, represents only a vulgarized, public version. When I deliberate in private, if it is true deliberation, I seek to reproduce in my own mind an analogue of a public debate. I try to imagine what analogies would be urged, what arguments made; I test the conclusion I am deliberating by imagining having to justify it to a skeptical but reasonable audience. My point, then, is that justification to and within a moral community is not some externalized version of an ideal of internal moral deliberation, but rather the ideal itself. This is *not* at all to say that the right or the good is what happens to be accepted in a particular moral community at a particular time, any more than the truth about matters of science is just what happens to be accepted by the scientific community — as if the way to find out what is good or true were to conduct an opinion survey. In a moral or a scientific community the good or the true are goals of inquiry. Were it not so, what would direct the inquiry of those within the community — surely not a search for their own consensus. The point is rather that justification to reasonable men and women pursuing the good or the true is a regulative ideal of the pursuit of moral or scientific truth.[63] And this is what one would expect, given the fact that moral discourse is carried on in a language that is a public language, with concepts which are public concepts. When I think even about the most private, the most personal matters, I cannot do so other than in such a public language.

These general considerations spell the limits of my ambition in offering a theory of liberty. Absolute certainty and objectivity are not possible. What I have tried to offer instead has been a sense of confidence in a process of learning, of learning the truth about ourselves and the world. This confidence determines what at bottom we owe each other (a decent minimum) and what are

---

[63] For an interesting discussion of this conception of scientific inquiry, see the account of C. S. Peirce's views in Bernard Williams, *Descartes — The Project of Pure Inquiry*, 244–49 (Harmondsworth, 1978).

the bounds of our private sphere. If the answers to these questions are certain enough so is our liberty. I believe our liberty is certain enough. What I cannot assure you of is that what we are certain of today is what we will be certain of tomorrow. But why should this discourage us? In the end the belief in liberty, as in truth, on which it in part depends, is an act of faith.

Equality of What?

AMARTYA SEN

THE TANNER LECTURE ON HUMAN VALUES

Delivered at
Stanford University

May 22, 1979

AMARTYA SEN is Drummond Professor of Political Economy at Oxford University and a Fellow of All Souls College. Professor Sen was born in India and studied at Calcutta and at Cambridge. He has taught at Calcutta, Cambridge, Delhi, and London, and also at Berkeley, Harvard, M.I.T., and Stanford. He is a Fellow of the British Academy, a Foreign Honorary Member of the American Academy of Arts and Sciences, and a Past President of the Econometric Society. His books include *Choice of Techniques*; *Collective Choice and Social Welfare*; *On Economic Inequality*; *Employment, Technology and Development*; *Poverty and Famines*; *Choice, Welfare and Measurement*; *Resources, Values and Development*; and *Commodities and Capabilities*. He has published articles in economics, philosophy, political science, decision theory, and history. A selection of Professor Sen's philosophical papers, including his Dewey Lectures (1985), will be shortly published by Columbia University Press and Basil Blackwell under the title *Well-being, Agency and Freedom*.

Discussions in moral philosophy have offered us a wide menu in answer to the question: equality of what? In this lecture I shall concentrate on three particular types of equality, viz., (i) utilitarian equality, (ii) total utility equality, and (iii) Rawlsian equality. I shall argue that all three have serious limitations, and that while they fail in rather different and contrasting ways, an adequate theory cannot be constructed even on the *combined* grounds of the three. Towards the end I shall try to present an alternative formulation of equality which seems to me to deserve a good deal more attention than it has received, and I shall not desist from doing some propaganda on its behalf.

First a methodological question. When it is claimed that a certain moral principle has shortcomings, what can be the basis of such an allegation? There seem to be at least two different ways of grounding such a criticism, aside from just checking its *direct* appeal to moral intuition. One is to check the *implications* of the principle by taking up particular cases in which the results of employing that principle can be seen in a rather stark way, and then to examine these implications against our intuition. I shall call such a critique a *case-implication critique*. The other is to move not from the general to the particular, but from the general to the *more* general. One can examine the consistency of the principle with another principle that is acknowledged to be more fundamental. Such prior principles are usually formulated at a rather abstract level, and frequently take the form of congruence with some very general procedures. For example, what could be reasonably assumed to have been chosen under the *as if* ignorance of the Rawlsian "original position," a hypothetical primordial

NOTE: For helpful comments I am most grateful to Derek Parfit, Jim Griffin, and John Perry.

state in which people decide on what rules to adopt without know-
ing who they are going to be — as if they could end up being any
one of the persons in the community.[1] Or what rules would satisfy
Richard Hare's requirement of "universalizability" and be consistent with "giving equal weights to the equal interests of the
occupants of all the roles."[2] I shall call a critique based on such
an approach a *prior-principle critique*. Both approaches can be
used in assessing the moral claims of each type of equality, and
will indeed be used here.

1. UTILITARIAN EQUALITY

Utilitarian equality is the equality that can be derived from
the utilitarian concept of goodness applied to problems of distribution. Perhaps the simplest case is the "pure distribution problem": the problem of dividing a given homogeneous cake among
a group of persons.[3] Each person gets more utility the larger his
share of the cake, and gets utility *only* from his share of the cake;
his utility increases at a diminishing rate as the amount of his
share goes up. The utilitarian objective is to maximize the sum-
total of utility irrespective of distribution, but that requires the
equality of the *marginal* utility of everyone — marginal utility
being the incremental utility each person would get from an addi-

[1] J. Rawls, *A Theory of Justice* (Cambridge: Harvard University Press, 1971),
pp. 17–22. See also W. Vickrey, 'Measuring Marginal Utility by Reactions to Risk',
Econometrica 13 (1945), and J. C. Harsanyi, 'Cardinal Welfare, Individualistic
Ethics, and Interpersonal Comparisons of Utility', *Journal of Political Economy* 63
(1955).

[2] R. M. Hare, *The Language of Morals* (Oxford: Clarendon Press, 1952); 'Ethical
Theory and Utilitarianism', in H. D. Lewis, ed., *Contemporary British Philosophy*
(London: Allen and Unwin, 1976), pp. 116–17.

[3] I have tried to use this format for an axiomatic contrast of the Rawlsian and
utilitarian criteria in 'Rawls versus Bentham: An Axiomatic Examination of the Pure
Distribution Problem', in *Theory and Decision* 4 (1974); reprinted in N. Daniels,
ed., *Reading Rawls* (Oxford: Blackwell, 1975). See also L. Kern, 'Comparative Distributive Ethics: An Extension of Sen's Examination of the Pure Distribution Problem', in H. W. Gottinger and W. Leinfellner, eds., *Decision Theory and Social Ethics*
(Dordrecht: Reidel, 1978), and J. P. Griffin, 'Equality: On Sen's Equity Axiom',
Keble College, Oxford, 1978, mimeographed.

tional unit of cake.[4] According to one interpretation, this equality of marginal utility embodies equal treatment of everyone's interests.[5]

The position is a bit more complicated when the total size of the cake is not independent of its distribution. But even then maximization of the total utility sum requires that transfers be carried to the point at which the marginal utility gain of the gainers equals the marginal utility loss of the losers, after taking into account the effect of the transfer on the size and distribution of the cake.[6] It is in this wider context that the special type of equality insisted upon by utilitarianism becomes assertively distinguished. Richard Hare has claimed that "giving equal weight to the equal interests of all the parties" would "lead to utilitarianism" — thus satisfying the prior-principle requirement of universalizability.[7] Similarly, John Harsanyi shoots down the non-utilitarians (including this lecturer, I hasten to add), by claiming for utilitarianism an exclusive ability to avoid "unfair discrimination" between "one person's and another person's equally urgent human needs."[8]

The moral importance of needs, on this interpretation, is based exclusively on the notion of utility. This is disputable, and having had several occasions to dispute it in the past,[9] I shall not shy away

---

[4] The equality condition would have to be replaced by a corresponding combination of inequality requirements when the appropriate "continuity" properties do not hold. Deeper difficulties are raised by "non-convexities" (e.g., increasing marginal utility).

[5] J. Harsanyi, 'Can the Maximin Principle Serve as a Basis for Morality? A Critique of John Rawls' Theory', *American Political Science Review* 64 (1975).

[6] As mentioned in footnote 4, the equality conditions would require modification in the absence of continuity of the appropriate type. Transfers must be carried to the point at which the marginal utility gain of the gainers from any further transfer is *no more than* the marginal utility loss of the losers.

[7] Hare (1976), pp. 116–17.

[8] John Harsanyi, 'Non-linear Social Welfare Functions: A Rejoinder to Professor Sen', in R. E. Butts and J. Hintikka, eds., *Foundational Problems in the Special Sciences* (Dordrecht: Reidel, 1977), pp. 294–95.

[9] *Collective Choice and Social Welfare* (San Francisco: Holden-Day, 1970), chapter 6 and section 11.4; 'On Weights and Measures: Informational Constraints in

from disputing it in this particular context. But while I will get on to this issue later, I want first to examine the nature of utilitarian equality without — for the time being — questioning the grounding of moral importance entirely on utility. Even when utility is the sole basis of importance there is still the question as to whether the size of *marginal* utility, irrespective of *total* utility enjoyed by the person, is an adequate index of moral importance. It is, of course, possible to define a metric on utility characteristics such that each person's utility scale is coordinated with everyone else's in a way that equal social importance is simply "scaled" as equal marginal utility. If interpersonal comparisons of utility are taken to have no descriptive content, then this can indeed be thought to be a natural approach. No matter how the relative social importances are arrived at, the marginal utilities attributed to each person would then simply reflect these values. This can be done explicitly by appropriate interpersonal scaling,[10] or implicitly through making the utility numbering reflect choices in situations of *as if* uncertainty associated with the "original position" under the additional assumption that ignorance be interpreted as equal probability of being anyone.[11] This is not the occasion to go into the technical details of this type of exercise, but the essence of it consists in using a scaling procedure such that marginal utility measures are automatically identified as indicators of social importance.

This route to utilitarianism may meet with little resistance, but it is non-controversial mainly because it says so little. A prob-

---

Social Welfare Analysis', *Econometrica* 45 (1977). See also T. M. Scanlon's arguments against identifying utility with "urgency" in his 'Preference and Urgency', *Journal of Philosophy* 72 (1975).

[10] For two highly ingenious examples of such an exercise, see Peter Hammond, 'Dual Interpersonal Comparisons of Utility and the Welfare Economics of Income Distribution', *Journal of Public Economics* 6 (1977): 51–57; and Menahem Yaari, 'Rawls, Edgeworth, Shapley and Nash: Theories of Distributive Justice Re-examined', Research Memorandum No. 33, Center for Research in Mathematical Economics and Game Theory, Hebrew University, Jerusalem, 1978.

[11] See Harsanyi (1955, 1975, 1977).

lem arises the moment utilities and interpersonal comparisons thereof are taken to have some independent descriptive content, as utilitarians have traditionally insisted that they do. There could then be conflicts between these descriptive utilities and the appropriately scaled, essentially normative, utilities in terms of which one is "forced" to be a utilitarian. In what follows I shall have nothing more to say on utilitarianism through appropriate interpersonal scaling, and return to examining the traditional utilitarian position, which takes utilities to have interpersonally comparable descriptive content. How moral importance should relate to these descriptive features must, then, be explicitly faced.

The position can be examined from the prior-principle perspective as well as from the case-implication angle. John Rawls's criticism as a preliminary to presenting his own alternative conception of justice took mostly the prior-principle form. This was chiefly in terms of acceptability in the "original position," arguing that in the postulated situation of *as if* ignorance people would not choose to maximize the utility sum. But Rawls also discussed the violence that utilitarianism does to our notions of liberty and equality. Some replies to Rawls's arguments have reasserted the necessity to be a utilitarian by taking the "scaling" route, which was discussed earlier, and which — I think — is inappropriate in meeting Rawls's critique. But I must confess that I find the lure of the "original position" distinctly resistible since it seems very unclear what precisely would be chosen in such a situation. It is also far from obvious that prudential choice under *as if* uncertainty provides an adequate basis for moral judgment in *un-*original, i.e., real-life, positions.[12] But I believe Rawls's more direct critiques in terms of liberty and equality do remain powerful.

Insofar as one is concerned with the *distribution* of utilities, it

---

[12] On this, see Thomas Nagel, 'Rawls on Justice', *Philosophical Review* 83 (1973), and 'Equality' in his *Mortal Questions* (Cambridge: Cambridge University Press, 1979).

follows immediately that utilitarianism would in general give one little comfort. Even the minutest gain in total utility *sum* would be taken to outweigh distributional inequalities of the most blatant kind. This problem would be avoidable under certain assumptions, notably the case in which everyone has the *same* utility function. In the pure distribution problem, with this assumption the utilitarian best would require absolute equality of everyone's total utilities.[13] This is because when the marginal utilities are equated, so would be the total utilities if everyone has the same utility function. This is, however, egalitarianism by serendipity: just the accidental result of the marginal tail wagging the total dog. More importantly, the assumption would be very frequently violated, since there are obvious and well-discussed variations between human beings. John may be easy to please, but Jeremy not. If it is taken to be an acceptable prior-principle that the equality of the distribution of total utilities has some value, then the utilitarian conception of equality — marginal as it is — must stand condemned.

The recognition of the fundamental diversity of human beings does, in fact, have very deep consequences, affecting not merely the utilitarian conception of social good, but others as well, including (as I shall argue presently) even the Rawlsian conception of equality. If human beings are identical, then the application of the prior-principle of universalizability in the form of "giving equal weight to the equal interest of all parties" simplifies enormously. Equal marginal utilities of all — reflecting one interpretation of the equal treatment of needs — coincides with equal total utilities — reflecting one interpretation of serving their overall interests equally well. With diversity, the two can pull in opposite directions, and it is far from clear that "giving equal weight to

---

[13] The problem is much more complex when the total cake is not fixed, and where the maximization of utility sum need not lead to the equality of total utilities unless some additional assumptions are made, e.g., the absence of incentive arguments for inequality.

the equal interest of all parties" would require us to concentrate only on one of the two parameters — taking no note of the other.

The case-implication perspective can also be used to develop a related critique, and I have tried to present such a critique elsewhere.[14] For example, if person A as a cripple gets half the utility that the pleasure-wizard person B does from any given level of income, then in the pure distribution problem between A and B the utilitarian would end up giving the pleasure-wizard B more income than the cripple A. The cripple would then be doubly worse off: both since he gets less utility from the same level of income, *and* since he will also get less income. Utilitarianism must lead to this thanks to its single-minded concern with maximizing the utility sum. The pleasure-wizard's superior efficiency in producing utility would pull income away from the less efficient cripple.

Since this example has been discussed a certain amount,[15] I should perhaps explain what is being asserted and what is not. First, it is *not* being claimed that anyone who has lower total utility (e.g., the cripple) at any given level of income must of necessity have lower marginal utility also. This must be true for some levels of income, but need not be true everywhere. Indeed, the opposite could be the case when incomes are equally distributed. If that were so, then of course even utilitarianism would give the cripple more income than the non-cripple, since at that point the cripple would be the more efficient producer of utility. My point is that there is no guarantee that this will be the case, and more particularly, if it were the case that the cripple were not only worse off in terms of total utility but could convert income into utility less efficiently everywhere (or even just at the point of

[14] *On Economic Inequality* (Oxford: Clarendon Press, 1973), pp. 16–20.

[15] See John Harsanyi, 'Non-linear Social Welfare Functions', *Theory and Decision* 6 (1976): 311–12; Harsanyi (1977); Kern (1978); Griffin (1978); Richard B. Brandt, *A Theory of the Good and the Right* (Oxford: Clarendon Press, 1979), chapter 16.

equal income division), then utilitarianism would compound his disadvantage by settling him with less income on top of lower efficiency in making utility out of income. The point, of course, is not about cripples in general, nor about all people with total utility disadvantage, but concerns people — including cripples — with disadvantage in terms of both total *and* marginal utility at the relevant points.

Second, the descriptive content of utility is rather important in this context. Obviously, if utilities were scaled to reflect moral importance, then wishing to give priority to income for the cripple would simply amount to attributing a higher "marginal utility" to the cripple's income; but this — as we have already discussed — is a very special sense of utility — quite devoid of descriptive content. In terms of descriptive features, what is being assumed in our example is that the cripple can be helped by giving him income, but the increase in his utility as a consequence of a marginal increase in income is less — in terms of the accepted descriptive criteria — than giving that unit of income to the pleasure-wizard, when both have initially the same income.

Finally, the problem for utilitarianism in this case-implication argument is not dependent on an implicit assumption that the claim to more income arising from disadvantage must dominate over the claim arising from high marginal utility.[16] A system that gives some weight to both claims would still fail to meet the utilitarian formula of social good, which demands an exclusive concern with the latter claim. It is this narrowness that makes the utilitarian conception of equality such a limited one. Even when utility is accepted as the only basis of moral importance, utilitarianism fails to capture the relevance of overall advantage for the requirements of equality. The prior-principle critiques can be supplemented by case-implication critiques using this utilitarian lack

16 Such an assumption is made in my Weak Equity Axiom, proposed in Sen (1973), but it is unnecessarily demanding for rejecting utilitarianism. See Griffin (1978) for a telling critique of the Weak Equity Axiom, in this exacting form.

of concern with distributional questions except at the entirely marginal level.

2. TOTAL UTILITY EQUALITY

Welfarism is the view that the goodness of a state of affairs can be judged entirely by the goodness of the utilities in that state.[17] This is a less demanding view than utilitarianism in that it does not demand — in addition — that the goodness of the utilities must be judged by their sum-total. Utilitarianism is, in this sense, a special case of welfarism, and provides one illustration of it. Another distinguished case is the criterion of judging the goodness of a state by the utility level of the worst-off person in that state — a criterion often attributed to John Rawls. (*Except* by John Rawls! He uses social primary goods rather than utility as the index of advantage, as we shall presently discuss.) One can also take some other function of the utilities — other than the sum-total or the minimal element.

Utilitarian equality is one type of welfarist equality. There are others, notably the equality of total utility. It is tempting to think of this as some kind of an analogue of utilitarianism shifting the focus from marginal utility to total utility. This correspondence is, however, rather less close than it might first appear. First of all, while we economists often tend to treat the marginal and the total as belonging to the same plane of discourse, there is an important difference between them. Marginal is an essentially *counter-factual* notion: marginal utility is the additional utility that *would be* generated if the person had one more unit of income. It contrasts what is observed with what allegedly would be observed if something else were different: in this case if the income had been one unit greater. Total is not, however, an inherently counter-factual concept; whether it is or is not would

[17] See Sen (1977), and also my 'Welfarism and Utilitarianism', *Journal of Philosophy* 76 (1979).

depend on the variable that is being totalled. In case of utilities, if they are taken to be observed facts, total utility will not be counter-factual. Thus total utility equality is a matter for direct observation, whereas utilitarian equality is not so, since the latter requires hypotheses as to what things would have been under different postulated circumstances. The contrast can be easily traced to the fact that utilitarian equality is essentially a consequence of sum *maximization*, which is itself a counter-factual notion, whereas total utility equality is an equality of some directly observed magnitudes.

Second, utilitarianism provides a complete ordering of all utility distributions — the ranking reflecting the order of the sums of individual utilities—but as specified so far, total utility equality does not do more than just point to the case of absolute equality. In dealing with two cases of non-equal distributions, something more has to be said so that they could be ranked. The ranking can be completed in many different ways.

One way to such a complete ranking is provided by the lexicographic version of the maximin rule, which is associated with the Rawlsian Difference Principle, but interpreted in terms of utilities as opposed to primary goods. Here the goodness of the state of affairs is judged by the level of utility of the worst-off person in that state; but if the worst-off persons in two states respectively have the same level of utility, then the states are ranked according to the utility levels of the second worst-off. If they too tie, then by the utility levels of the third worst-off, and so on. And if two utility distributions are matched at each rank all the way from the worst off to the best off, then the two distributions are equally good. Following a convention established in social choice theory, I shall call this *leximin*.

In what way does total utility equality lead to the leximin? It does this when combined with some other axioms, and in fact the analysis closely parallels the recent axiomatic derivations of

the Difference Principle by several authors.[18] Consider four utility
levels *a*, *b*, *c*, *d*, in decreasing order of magnitude. One can argue
that in an obvious sense the pair of extreme points (a, d) displays
greater inequality than the pair of intermediate points (b, c).
Note that this is a purely *ordinal* comparison based on ranking
only, and the exact magnitudes of *a*, *b*, *c*, and *d* make no difference
to the comparison in question. If one were *solely* concerned with
equality, then it could be argued that (b, c) is superior — or at
least non-inferior — to (a, d). This requirement may be seen as
a strong version of preferring equality of utility distributions, and
may be called "utility equality preference." It is possible to combine this with an axiom due to Patrick Suppes which captures the
notion of *dominance* of one utility distribution over another, in
the sense of each element of one distribution being at least as
large as the corresponding element in the other distribution.[19]
In the two-person case this requires that state *x* must be regarded
as at least as good as *y*, *either* if each person in state *x* has at least
as much utility as himself in state *y*, *or* if each person in state *x*
has at least as much utility as the *other* person in state *y*. If, in
addition, at least one of them has strictly more, then of course *x*
could be declared to be strictly better (and not merely at least as
good). If this Suppes principle and the "utility equality preference" are combined, then we are pushed in the direction of
leximin. Indeed, leximin can be fully derived from these two
principles by requiring that the approach must provide a com-

---

[18] See P. J. Hammond, 'Equity, Arrow's Conditions and Rawls' Difference Principle', *Econometrica* 44 (1976); S. Strasnick, 'Social Choice Theory and the Derivation
of Rawls' Difference Principle', *Journal of Philosophy* 73 (1976); C. d'Aspremont
and L. Gevers, 'Equity and Informational Basis of Collective Choice', *Review of Economic Studies* 44 (1977); K. J. Arrow, 'Extended Sympathy and the Possibility of
Social Choice', *American Economic Review* 67 (1977); A. K. Sen, 'On Weights and
Measures: Informational Constraints in Social Welfare Analysis', *Econometrica* 45
(1977); R. Deschamps and L. Gevers, 'Leximin and Utilitarian Rules: A Joint Characterization', *Journal of Economic Theory* 17 (1978); K. W. S. Roberts, 'Possibility
Theorems with Interpersonally Comparable Welfare Levels', *Review of Economic
Studies* 47 (1980); P. J. Hammond, 'Two Person Equity', *Econometrica* 47 (1979).

[19] P. Suppes, 'Some Formal Models of Grading Principles', *Synthese* 6 (1966).

plete ordering of all possible states no matter what the interpersonally comparable individual utilities happen to be (called
"unrestricted domain"), and that the ranking of any two states
must depend on utility information concerning *those* states only
(called "independence").

Insofar as the requirements other than utility equality preference (i.e., the Suppes principle, unrestricted domain, and independence) are regarded as acceptable — and they have indeed
been widely used in the social choice literature — leximin can
be seen as the natural concomitant of giving priority to the conception of equality focussing on total utility.

It should be obvious, however, that leximin can be fairly easily
criticised from the prior-principle perspective as well as the case-
implication perspective. Just as utilitarianism pays no attention
to the force of one's claim arising from one's disadvantage, leximin ignores claims arising from the *intensity* of one's needs. The
ordinal characteristic that was pointed out while presenting the
axiom of utility equality preference makes the approach insensi-
tive to the magnitudes of potential utility gains and losses.
While in the critique of utilitarianism that was presented earlier
I argued against treating these potential gains and losses as the
only basis of moral judgment, it was *not* of course alleged that
these have no moral relevance at all. Take the comparison of
(a, d) vis-a-vis (b, c), discussed earlier, and let (b, c) stand for
$(3, 2)$. Utility equality preference would assert the superiority of
$(3, 2)$ over $(10, 1)$ as well as $(4, 1)$. Indeed, it would not distinguish between the two cases at all. It is this lack of concern
with "how much" questions that makes leximin rather easy to criti-
cise *either* by showing its failure to comply with such prior-
principles as "giving equal weight to the equal interest of all
parties," *or* by spelling out its rather austere implications in
specific cases.

Aside from its indifference to "how much" questions, leximin
also has little interest in "how many" questions — paying no

attention at all to the number of people whose interests are over-ridden in the pursuit of the interests of the worst off. The worst-off position rules the roost, and it does not matter whether this goes against the interests of one other person, or against those of a million or a billion other persons. It is sometimes claimed that leximin would not be such an extreme criterion if it could be modified so that this innumeracy were avoided, and if the interests of *one* worse-off position were given priority over the interests of exactly *one* better-off position, but not necessarily against the interests of *more than one* better-off position. In fact, one can define a less demanding version of leximin, which can be called leximin-2, which takes the form of applying the leximin principle *if* all persons other than two are indifferent between the alterna-tives, but not necessarily otherwise. Leximin-2, as a compromise, will be still unconcerned with "how much" questions on the magnitudes of utilities of the two non-indifferent persons, but need not be blinkered about "how many" questions dealing with numbers of people: the priority applies to one person over exactly one other.[20]

Interestingly enough, a consistency problem intervenes here. It can be proved that given the regularity conditions, viz., un-restricted domain and independence, leximin-2 logically entails leximin in general.[21] That is, given these regularity conditions, there is no way of retaining moral sensitivity to the number of people on each side by choosing the limited requirement of leximin-2 without going all the way to leximin itself. It appears that indifference to *how much* questions concerning utilities im-plies indifference to *how many* questions concerning the number of

[20] Leximin — and maximin — are concerned with conflicts between positional priorities, i.e., between ranks (such as the "worst-off position," "second worst-off posi-tion," etc.), and not with interpersonal priorities. When positions coincide with per-sons (e.g., the *same* person being the worst off in each state), then positional conflicts translate directly into personal conflicts.

[21] Theorem 8, Sen (1977). See also Hammond (1979) for extensions of this result.

people on different sides. One innumeracy begets another.

Given the nature of these critiques of utilitarian equality and total utility equality respectively, it is natural to ask whether some *combination* of the two should not meet both sets of objections. If utilitarianism is attacked for its unconcern with inequalities of the utility distribution, and leximin is criticised for its lack of interest in the magnitudes of utility gains and losses, and even in the numbers involved, then isn't the right solution to choose some mixture of the two? It is at this point that the long-postponed question of the relation between utility and moral worth becomes crucial. While utilitarianism and leximin differ sharply from each other in the use that they respectively make of the utility information, both share an exclusive concern with utility data. If non-utility considerations have any role in either approach, this arises from the part they play in the determination of utilities, or possibly as surrogates for utility information in the absence of adequate utility data. A combination of utilitarianism and leximin would still be confined to the box of welfarism, and it remains to be examined whether welfarism as a general approach is *itself* adequate.

One aspect of the obtuseness of welfarism was discussed clearly by John Rawls.

In calculating the greatest balance of satisfaction it does not matter, except indirectly, what the desires are for. We are to arrange institutions so as to obtain the greatest sum of satisfactions; we ask no questions about their source or quality but only how their satisfaction would affect the total of well-being. . . . Thus if men take a certain pleasure in discriminating against one another, in subjecting others to a lesser liberty as a means of enhancing their self-respect, then the satisfaction of these desires must be weighed in our deliberations according to their intensity, or whatever, along with other desires. . . . In justice as fairness, on the other hand, persons accept in advance a principle of equal liberty and they do this without a knowledge of their more particular ends. . . . An individual who finds that he enjoys seeing others in positions of lesser liberty understands that he has no claim whatever to this enjoyment. The pleasure he takes in other's deprivation is wrong in itself: it is a satisfaction which requires the violation of a principle to which he would agree in the original position.[22]

It is easily seen that this is an argument not merely against utilitarianism, but against the adequacy of utility information for moral judgments of states of affairs, and is, thus, an attack on welfarism in general. Second, it is clear that as a criticism of welfarism — and *a fortiori* as a critique of utilitarianism — the argument uses a principle that is unnecessarily strong. If it were the case that pleasures taken "in other's deprivation" were not taken to be wrong in itself, but simply *disregarded*, even then the rejection of welfarism would stand. Furthermore, even if such pleasures were regarded as valuable, but *less* valuable than pleasures arising from other sources (e.g., enjoying food, work, or leisure), welfarism would still stand rejected. The issue — as John Stuart Mill had noted — is the lack of "parity" between one source of utility and another.[23] Welfarism requires the endorsement not merely of the widely shared intuition that any pleasure has some value — and one would have to be a bit of a kill-joy to dissent from this — but also the much more dubious proposition that pleasures must be relatively weighed *only* according to their respective intensities, irrespective of the source of the pleasure and the nature of the activity that goes with it. Finally, Rawls's argument takes the form of an appeal to the prior-principle of equating moral rightness with prudential acceptability in the original position. Even those who do not accept that prior principle could reject the welfarist no-nonsense counting of utility irrespective of all other information by reference to other prior principles, e.g., the irreducible value of liberty.

[22] Rawls (1971), pp. 30–31.
[23] John Stuart Mill, *On Liberty* (1859), p. 140.

The relevance of non-utility information to moral judgments is the central issue involved in disputing welfarism. Libertarian considerations point towards a particular class of non-utility information, and I have argued elsewhere that this may require even the rejection of the so-called Pareto principle based on utility dominance.[24] But there are also other types of non-utility information which have been thought to be intrinsically important. Tim Scanlon has recently discussed the contrast between "urgency" and utility (or intensity of preference). He has also argued that "the criteria of well-being that we actually employ in making moral judgments are objective," and a person's level of well-being is taken to be "independent of that person's tastes and interests."[25] These moral judgments could thus conflict with utilitarian — and more generally (Scanlon could have argued) with welfarist — moralities, no matter whether utility is interpreted as pleasure, or — as is increasingly common recently — as desire-fulfilment.

However, acknowledging the relevance of objective factors does not require that well-being be taken to be independent of tastes, and Scanlon's categories are *too* pure. For example, a lack of "parity" between utility from self-regarding actions and that from other-regarding actions will go beyond utility as an index of well-being and will be fatal to welfarism, but the contrast is not, of course, independent of tastes and subjective features. "Objective" considerations can count along with a person's tastes. What is required is the denial that a person's well-being be judged *exclusively* in terms of his or her utilities. If such judgments take into account a person's pleasures and desire-fulfilments, but also certain objective factors, e.g., whether he or she is hungry, cold, or oppressed, the resulting calculus would still be non-welfarist. Welfarism is an extremist position, and its denial can take many different forms — pure and mixed — so long as totally ignoring non-utility information is avoided.

---

[24] Sen (1970), especially chapter 6. Also Sen (1979).
[25] T. M. Scanlon (1975), pp. 658–59.

Second, it is also clear that the notion of urgency need not work only *through* the determinants of personal well-being — however broadly conceived. For example, the claim that one should not be *exploited* at work is not based on making exploitation an additional parameter in the specification of well-being on top of such factors as income and effort, but on the moral view that a person deserves to get what he — according to one way of characterizing production — has produced. Similarly, the urgency deriving from principles such as "equal pay for equal work" hits directly at discrimination without having to redefine the notion of personal well-being to take note of such discriminations. One could, for example, say: "She must be paid just as much as the men working in that job, not primarily because she would otherwise have a lower level of well-being than the others, but simply because she is doing the *same* work as the men there, and why should she be paid less?" These moral claims, based on non-welfarist conceptions of equality, have played important parts in social movements, and it seems difficult to sustain the hypothesis that they are purely "instrumental" claims — ultimately justified by their indirect impact on the fulfilment of welfarist, or other well-being-based, objectives.

Thus the dissociation of urgency from utility can arise from two different sources. One disentangles the notion of personal well-being from utility, and the other makes urgency not a function only of well-being. But, at the same time, the former does not require that well-being be independent of utility, and the latter does not necessitate a notion of urgency that is independent of personal well-being. Welfarism is a purist position and must avoid any contamination from either of these sources.

3. Rawlsian Equality

Rawls's "two principles of justice" characterize the need for equality in terms of — what he has called — "primary social goods." [26] These are "things that every rational man is presumed to want," including "rights, liberties and opportunities, income and wealth, and the social bases of self-respect." Basic liberties are separated out as having priority over other primary goods, and thus priority is given to the principle of liberty which demands that "each person is to have an equal right to the most extensive basic liberty compatible with a similar liberty for others." The second principle supplements this, demanding efficiency and equality, judging advantage in terms of an index of primary goods. Inequalities are condemned unless they work out to everyone's advantage. This incorporates the "Difference Principle" in which priority is given to furthering the interests of the worst-off. And that leads to maximin, or to leximin, defined not on individual utilities but on the index of primary goods. But given the priority of the liberty principle, no trade-offs are permitted between basic liberties and economic and social gain.

Herbert Hart has persuasively disputed Rawls's arguments for the priority of liberty,[27] but with that question I shall not be concerned in this lecture. What is crucial for the problem under discussion is the concentration on bundles of primary social goods. Some of the difficulties with welfarism that I tried to discuss will not apply to the pursuit of Rawlsian equality. Objective criteria of well-being can be directly accommodated within the index of primary goods. So can be Mill's denial of the parity between pleasures from different sources, since the sources can be discriminated on the basis of the nature of the goods. Furthermore, while the Difference Principle is egalitarian in a way similar to leximin, it avoids the much-criticised feature of leximin of giving more income to people who are hard to please and who have to be deluged in champagne and buried in caviar to bring them to a

26 Rawls (1971), pp. 60–65.

27 H. L. A. Hart, 'Rawls on Liberty and Its Priority', *University of Chicago Law Review* 40 (1973); reprinted in N. Daniels, ed., *Reading Rawls* (Oxford: Blackwell, 1975).

normal level of utility, which you and I get from a sandwich and beer. Since advantage is judged not in terms of utilities at all, but through the index of primary goods, expensive tastes cease to provide a ground for getting more income. Rawls justifies this in terms of a person's responsibility for his own ends.

But what about the cripple with utility disadvantage, whom we discussed earlier? Leximin will give him more income in a pure distribution problem. Utilitarianism, I had complained, will give him *less*. The Difference Principle will give him neither more nor less on grounds of his being a cripple. His utility disadvantage will be irrelevant to the Difference Principle. This may seem hard, and I think it is. Rawls justifies this by pointing out that "hard cases" can "distract our moral perception by leading us to think of people distant from us whose fate arouses pity and anxiety." [28] This can be so, but hard cases do exist, and to take disabilities, or special health needs, or physical or mental defects, as morally irrelevant, or to leave them out for fear of making a mistake, may guarantee that the *opposite* mistake will be made.

And the problem does not end with hard cases. The primary goods approach seems to take little note of the diversity of human beings. In the context of assessing utilitarian equality, it was argued that if people were fundamentally similar in terms of utility functions, then the utilitarian concern with maximizing the sum-total of utilities would push us simultaneously also in the direction of equality of utility levels. Thus utilitarianism could be rendered vastly more attractive if people really were similar. A corresponding remark can be made about the Rawlsian Difference Principle. If people were basically very similar, then an index of primary goods might be quite a good way of judging advantage. But, in fact, people seem to have very different needs varying with health, longevity, climatic conditions, location, work

[28] John Rawls, 'A Kantian Concept of Equality', *Cambridge Review* (February 1975), p. 96.

conditions, temperament, and even body size (affecting food and clothing requirements). So what is involved is not merely ignoring a few hard cases, but overlooking very widespread and real differences. Judging advantage purely in terms of primary goods leads to a partially blind morality.

Indeed, it can be argued that there is, in fact, an element of "fetishism" in the Rawlsian framework. Rawls takes primary goods as the embodiment of advantage, rather than taking advantage to be a *relationship* between persons and goods. Utilitarianism, or leximin, or — more generally — welfarism does not have this fetishism, since utilities are reflections of one type of relation between persons and goods. For example, income and wealth are not valued under utilitarianism as physical units, but in terms of their capacity to create human happiness or to satisfy human desires. Even if utility is not thought to be the right focus for the person–good relationship, to have an entirely good-oriented framework provides a peculiar way of judging advantage.

It can also be argued that while utility in the form of happiness or desire-fulfilment may be an *inadequate* guide to urgency, the Rawlsian framework asserts it to be *irrelevant* to urgency, which is, of course, a much stronger claim. The distinction was discussed earlier in the context of assessing welfarism, and it was pointed out that a rejection of welfarism need not take us to the point in which utility is given no role whatsoever. That a person's interest should have nothing directly to do with his happiness or desire-fulfilment seems difficult to justify. Even in terms of the prior-principle of prudential acceptability in the "original position," it is not at all clear why people in that primordial state should be taken to be so indifferent to the joys and sufferings in occupying particular positions, or if they are not, why their concern about these joys and sufferings should be taken to be morally irrelevant.

4. BASIC CAPABILITY EQUALITY

This leads to the further question: Can we not construct an adequate theory of equality on the *combined* grounds of Rawlsian equality and equality under the two welfarist conceptions, with some trade-offs among them. I would now like to argue briefly why I believe this too may prove to be informationally short. This can, of course, easily be asserted *if* claims arising from considerations other than well-being were acknowledged to be legitimate. Non-exploitation, or non-discrimination, requires the use of information not fully captured either by utility or by primary goods. Other conceptions of entitlements can also be brought in going beyond concern with personal well-being only. But in what follows I shall not introduce these concepts. My contention is that *even* the concept of *needs* does not get adequate coverage through the information on primary goods and utility.

I shall use a case-implication argument. Take the cripple again with marginal utility disadvantage. We saw that utilitarianism would do nothing for him; in fact it will give him *less* income than to the physically fit. Nor would the Difference Principle help him; it will leave his physical disadvantage severely alone. He did, however, get preferential treatment under leximin, and more generally, under criteria fostering total equality. His low level of total utility was the basis of his claim. But now suppose that he is no worse off than others in utility terms despite his physical handicap because of certain other utility features. This could be because he has a jolly disposition. Or because he has a low aspiration level and his heart leaps up whenever he sees a rainbow in the sky. Or because he is religious and feels that he will be rewarded in after-life, or cheerfully accepts what he takes to be just penalty for misdeeds in a past incarnation. The important point is that despite his marginal utility disadvantage, he has no longer a total utility deprivation. Now not even leximin — or any other notion of equality focussing on total utility — will do much for him. If we still think that he has needs as a cripple that should be catered to, then the basis of that claim clearly rests neither in high marginal utility, nor in low total utility, nor — of course — in deprivation in terms of primary goods.

It is arguable that what is missing in all this framework is some notion of "basic capabilities": a person being able to do certain basic things. The ability to move about is the relevant one here, but one can consider others, e.g., the ability to meet one's nutritional requirements, the wherewithal to be clothed and sheltered, the power to participate in the social life of the community. The notion of urgency related to this is not fully captured by either utility or primary goods, or any combination of the two. Primary goods suffers from fetishist handicap in being concerned with goods, and even though the list of goods is specified in a broad and inclusive way, encompassing rights, liberties, opportunities, income, wealth, and the social basis of self-respect, it still is concerned with good things rather than with what these good things *do* to human beings. Utility, on the other hand, *is* concerned with what these things do to human beings, but uses a metric that focusses not on the person's capabilities but on his mental reaction. There is something still missing in the combined list of primary goods and utilities. If it is argued that resources should be devoted to remove or substantially reduce the handicap of the cripple despite there being no marginal utility argument (because it is expensive), despite there being no total utility argument (because he is so contented), and despite there being no primary goods deprivation (because he has the goods that others have), the case must rest on something else. I believe what is at issue is the interpretation of needs in the form of basic capabilities. This interpretation of needs and interests is often implicit in the demand for equality. This type of equality I shall call "basic capability equality."

The focus on basic capabilities can be seen as a natural extension of Rawls's concern with primary goods, shifting attention from goods to what goods do to human beings. Rawls himself motivates judging advantage in terms of primary goods by referring to capabilities, even though his criteria end up focussing on goods as such: on income rather than on what income does, on the "social bases of self-respect" rather than on self-respect itself, and so on. If human beings were very like each other, this would not have mattered a great deal, but there is evidence that the conversion of goods to capabilities varies from person to person substantially, and the equality of the former may still be far from the equality of the latter.

There are, of course, many difficulties with the notion of "basic capability equality." In particular, the problem of indexing the basic capability bundles is a serious one. It is, in many ways, a problem comparable with the indexing of primary good bundles in the context of Rawlsian equality. This is not the occasion to go into the technical issues involved in such an indexing, but it is clear that whatever partial ordering can be done on the basis of broad uniformity of personal preferences must be supplemented by certain established conventions of relative importance.

The ideas of relative importance are, of course, conditional on the nature of the society. The notion of the equality of basic capabilities is a very general one, but any application of it must be rather culture-dependent, especially in the weighting of different capabilities. While Rawlsian equality has the characteristic of being both culture-dependent and fetishist, basic capability equality avoids fetishism, but remains culture-dependent. Indeed, basic capability equality can be seen as essentially an extension of the Rawlsian approach in a non-fetishist direction.

5. CONCLUDING REMARKS

I end with three final remarks. First, it is not my contention that basic capability equality can be the sole guide to the moral good. For one thing morality is not concerned only with equality.

For another, while it is my contention that basic capability equality has certain clear advantages over other types of equality, I did not argue that the others were morally irrelevant. Basic capability equality is a partial guide to the part of moral goodness that is associated with the idea of equality. I have tried to argue that as a partial guide it has virtues that the other characterisations of equality do not possess.

Second, the index of basic capabilities, like utility, can be used in many different ways. Basic capability equality corresponds to total utility equality, and it can be extended in different directions, e.g., to leximin of basic capabilities. On the other hand, the index can be used also in a way similar to utilitarianism, judging the strength of a claim in terms of incremental contribution to *enhancing* the index value. The main departure is in focussing on a *magnitude* different from utility as well as the primary goods index. The new dimension can be utilised in different ways, of which basic capability equality is only one.

Last, the bulk of this lecture has been concerned with rejecting the claims of utilitarian equality, total utility equality, and Rawlsian equality to provide a sufficient basis for the equality-aspect of morality — indeed, even for that part of it which is concerned with needs rather than deserts. I have argued that none of these three is sufficient, nor is any combination of the three.

This is my main thesis. I have also made the constructive claim that this gap can be narrowed by the idea of basic capability equality, and more generally by the use of basic capability as a morally relevant dimension taking us beyond utility and primary goods. I should end by pointing out that the validity of the main thesis is not conditional on the acceptance of this constructive claim.

Ethics, Law, and the Exercise of Self-Command

THOMAS C. SCHELLING

THE TANNER LECTURES ON HUMAN VALUES

Delivered at
The University of Michigan

March 19 and 21, 1982

THOMAS C. SCHELLING did his graduate work at Harvard University immediately after World War II and joined the Marshall Plan, first in Europe and then in Washington, D.C. He taught at Yale University for five years, and became Professor of Economics at Harvard in 1958. Most of his work has been in the study of bargaining and conflict, much of it applied to diplomacy, strategy, and arms control. A special interest has been the unintended collective consequences of individually purposive behavior. *The Strategy of Conflict* and *Micromotives and Macrobehavior* reflect these interests. Recently he has turned his attention to the ways people try to control their own behavior, and some of the policy issues in self-management.

A few years ago I saw again, after nearly fifty years, the original *Moby Dick*, an early talkie in black and white. Ahab, in a bunk below deck after his leg is severed by the whale, watches the ship's blacksmith approach with a red-hot iron which, only slightly cooled by momentary immersion in a bucket of water, is to cauterize his stump. As three seamen hold him he pleads not to be burnt, begging in horror as the blacksmith throws back the blanket. And as the iron touches his body he spews out the apple that he has been chewing, in the most awful scream that at age twelve I had ever heard.

Nobody doubts that the sailors who held him did what they had to do, and the blacksmith too. When the story resumes there is no sign that he regrets having been cauterized or bears any grievance toward the men who, rather than defend him against the hot iron, held him at the blacksmith's mercy.

They were not protecting him from an involuntary reflex. And he was not unaware of the medical consequences of an uncauterized wound. Until the iron touched him he knew exactly what was afoot. It was a moment of truth. He was unmistakably all there. He made his petition in clear and understandable language. They had neither personal interest nor legal obligation to subject him to torture. And they disregarded his plea.

When the iron struck he went out of his mind, still able, though, to communicate with perfect fidelity that all he wanted was the pain to stop. While the iron was burning his body we might declare him to have been not fully present, but until that instant it is hard to claim that he didn't understand better than we do what the stakes were.

* * *

Ahab and his wound dramatize a phenomenon that, usually not so terrifying, all of us have observed in others and most have observed in ourselves. It is behaving as if two selves were alternately in command. A familiar example is someone who cannot get up when the alarm goes off. More poignant is someone who cannot commit suicide.

I say only that people act *as if* there were two selves alternately in command. I'd rather not commit myself on whether there really are two different selves or cognitive faculties or value centers that alternate and compete for control. But the ways that people cope, or try to cope, with loss of command within or over themselves are much like the ways in which one exercises command over a second individual. Putting the alarm clock across the room is a familiar example. The varied behaviors and decisions that can display this quality range from merely troublesome to deadly serious:

— smoking, drinking, using drugs
— gambling
— scratching
— eating
— beating children while drunk
— procrastinating
— attempting suicide
— exercising
— diving off a high board
— staying awake
— panicking
— having stage fright
— spending on binges
— being sexually aroused

Let me try to be precise about what I have in mind. I shall state what it is and contrast it with some things that it isn't.

What I have in mind is an act or decision that a person takes decisively at some particular point in time, about which the person's preferences differ at the time of action from what they were earlier, when the prospect was contemplated but the decision was still in the future. If the person could make the final decision about that action at the earlier time, precluding a later change in mind, he would make a different choice from what he knows will be his choice on that later occasion.

Specifically, if I could decide now not to eat dessert at dinner, not to smoke a cigarette with my coffee, not to have a second glass of wine, and not to watch the late movie after I get home, I would make those decisions because *now* I want *not* to do those things *then*. And I know that when the time arrives I shall want to do those things and will do them. I now prefer to frustrate my later preferences.

Finding ways to anticipate those decisions, to make them irreversibly with the preferences of this moment and not leave them to be made differently when other preferences reign, can be difficult or impossible. *Decision theory* is the science of choosing in accordance with one's existing preferences, maximizing the satisfaction of one's values. When the values that govern one's preferences are liable to displacement by values that one deprecates, we need in addition something that we might call *command theory* — the theory of self-command, or self-management.[1]

Let me be clear about what I do not have in mind. People can undergo changes in mood. They like different foods at breakfast and at dinner. There are times when they want to hear music, other times when they want to talk, to be alone, to play with children, to play golf, or to go to bed. One can be a warrior during the day and a romantic at night, or absorbed in a laboratory for days on end and then spend a weekend above timberline. These are not unstable values. Even when someone is described as "a different person" in the evening from what he was during the day, or after a good night's sleep, the different persons are not in a quarrel with each other. If the warrior cannot savor, during the

---

[1] Some of the ways that people cope with themselves, or try to, are explored in Schelling, "The Intimate Contest for Self-Command," *The Public Interest* (Summer 1980), pp. 94–118.

heat of battle, the gentler nocturnal sport that requires a different mood, he can remember it when he needs to, can appreciate it, and can be sure that when the time comes his mood will respond.

The alternate moods do not discredit each other. They do not deny each other's legitimacy. A conscientious adult is able to allocate resources among these alternating activities and to be considerate of one mood while in another. The fact that my interest in dinner is at a nadir after breakfast does not mean that, asked what I want for dinner, I shall give a negligent answer. Just as a parent can allocate benefits among children, one can be one's own manager or referee and maintain a long-run perspective on his own biorhythms, changing moods, and seasonal interests, and not see the alternating moods and interests as contradictions. In economics this is the normal case. Decision theory treats people as able to mediate among points in time.

The contrast between this normal case and the case that I introduced with Ahab is that in deciding this morning what I would choose for this evening, or during summer whether to reserve a ski holiday eight months later, I normally want my preferences at that later time to be controlling. Those later preferences, as best I can anticipate them, are the ones that matter to me now. They may compete with the present, if my budget will cover only a seashore holiday this week or a ski holiday next winter, or if I cannot enjoy Sunday a movie that I already saw Wednesday. But however much those anticipated future preferences about a future action compete for resources with my current preferences about current action, my *current* preferences about that *future* occasion are those future preferences as I foresee them and appreciate them now. There can be competition but there is no conflict.

In this normal case I know that I shall want to watch the movie on television tonight and I make sure there is TV in my hotel room. In the other case I know that I shall want to watch the movie and for that reason I ask for a room without television. (I would even pay extra for a room with the TV disconnected.)

The phenomenon, then, that I want to deal with can be described as alternating preferences, or alternating values that are incompatible or uncompromisable. In the normal case there is a dynamic programming self that looks over wants and desires that continually change, anticipating preferences and attempting to satisfy them. It is as if there were a succession of momentary selves, each with its own wants and desires, all under the supervision of a timeless superself, an overall manager or referee who treats the transient selves evenhandedly.

In the case I want to discuss, that superself, that dynamically programming referee, does not exist. Instead, there is a succession or alternation of impermanent selves, each in command part of the time, each with its own needs and desires during the time it is in command, but having — at least some of them — strong preferences about what is done during the period that another one is in command. One of us, the nicotine addict, wants to smoke when he is in command; the other, concerned about health and longevity, wants not to smoke ever, no matter who is in command, and therefore wants *now* not to smoke *then* when he will want to. In the normal case a person's sexual interests wax and wane and, subject to the difficulty of imagining or remembering the alternate appetites, one tries to accommodate them; the case that concerns me is the person who some of the time wants sexual satisfaction and the rest of the time wants to be a virgin.[2]

* * *

[2] The richest, most varied, and most comprehensive approach to this subject that I have discovered is George Ainslie's "Specious Reward: A Behavioral Theory of Impulsiveness and Impulse Control," *Psychological Bulletin* 82 (July 1975), pp. 463–496, and some later unpublished work of Ainslie's. An intriguing philosophical approach to these issues is Jon Elster's "Ulysses and the Sirens: A Theory of Imperfect Rationality," *Social Science Information* 41 (1977), pp. 469–526, and his book *Ulysses and the Sirens*, mentioned in note 5. In economics there are attempts to accommodate self-management or self-control within traditional consumer theory and, more recently, some efforts to break out of the tradition. A pioneer work was Robert H. Strotz, "Myopia and Inconsistency in Dynamic Utility Maximization," *Review of Economic Studies* (1955–56), pp. 165–80. The best-known effort to fit this subject within the economics tradition is George J. Stigler

I have tried to describe a phenomenon that generates the problem of self-command, or self-management. Self-management is
not unilateral. It occurs in a social environment. People are helped
or hindered in their self-management by social arrangements. They
have friends who offer cigarettes and friends who chide them
when they smoke, hostesses who tempt them with chocolate and
hostesses who cooperate with an earlier self by serving grapefruit,
firms that advertise temptations and fraternities that support
abstinence. There are prohibitions, taxes, regulations, and public
education that impinge on self-management. Custom and etiquette
are involved. Work environments make a difference. Even stran-
gers can help.

The questions I want to call attention to are those of ethics
and social policy. If somebody now wants our help later in con-
straining his later behavior against his own wishes at that later
time, how do we decide which side we are on? If we promise now
to frustrate him later, and he later releases us from the very promise that we were to honor despite his release, must we — may
we — keep our promise against his express wishes? Should we
rescue Ahab from his tormentors? Should people be able to surrender to a "fat farm" that legally may keep them, or legally must
keep them, until their weight loss reaches the pounds they speci-

---

and Gary S. Becker, "De Gustibus Non Est Disputandum," *American Economic
Review* 67 (March 1977), pp. 76–90; their formulation denies the phenomenon I
discuss. On the edge of traditional economics are C. C. von Weizsacker, "Notes on
Endogenous Change of Tastes," *Journal of Economic Theory* (December 1971),
pp. 345–72, and Roger A. McCain, "Reflections on the Cultivations of Taste," *Journal of Cultural Economics* 3 (June 1979), pp. 30–52. Outside the tradition, and
viewing the consumer as complex rather than singular, are Amartya K. Sen, "Rational Fools: A Critique of the Behavioral Foundations of Economic Theory," *Philosophy and Public Affairs* 6 (Summer 1977), pp. 317–45; Gordon C. Winston,
"Addiction and Backsliding: A Theory of Compulsive Consumption," *Journal of
Economic Behavior and Organization*; and Howard Margolis, *Selfishness, Altruism,
and Rationality* (Cambridge University Press, 1982). Winston and Margolis recognize the referee, or superself, that I find lacking; whether the difference is one of
perception or of methodology I am not sure. The only genuinely multidisciplinary
work of any great scope by an economist that I know of is Tibor Scitovsky's brilliant
small book *The Joyless Economy: An Inquiry into Human Satisfaction and Consumer Dissatisfaction* (New York: Oxford University Press, 1976).

fied when they entered captivity? May a majority of the voting population ban dessert in the dining room, or outlaw cigarettes throughout the nation, not to keep others from eating or smoking but to discipline themselves?

In the cases that come quickly to mind, a conscientious bystander has little difficulty deciding which side he is on, between the two rival selves that occur in a friend or stranger. We excuse or discount what is said or done in anger, under stress or the influence of alcohol. We are expected to protect a drunk person from excessively generous as well as destructive impulses, to impede any momentous and irreversible action like giving all his money away, joining the foreign legion, or quitting his job. When begged for a cigarette by someone who we know is trying to quit, or asked for his car keys by someone who is drunk when it's time to go home, we may comply, but not without guilt. And we don't hesitate to be forceful with someone who will be late for work if he doesn't get out of bed.

But not all cases offer an easy choice. People trying to lose weight do not receive universal sympathy. A mother is expected to consider it unhealthy for a daughter to starve herself to be skinny, and she and her daughter may have different definitions of skinny. When the fear of fat takes on the proportions of a phobia, as among anorexic girls who learned to control their food intake by vomiting and are unable now not to vomit, our usual sympathy for abstinence gets a challenge. The dilemma is most poignant in deciding one's obligation when an opportunity presents itself to frustrate an attempt at suicide.

Still, the frequent and familiar cases usually seem to be easy cases, not hard ones. It may be hard to decide how far our obligation extends to someone who asks in advance that we use all necessary force when he has drunk too much to see that he does not become too candid in public about his wife or his employer or his host, or to keep him from driving his own car, or to keep him from drinking any more; but whatever obligation we feel is usually to that earlier self that asked our help and elicited a promise, the one to whom we have to explain our own behavior tomorrow when he's sober, and not the one who tells us to ignore the earlier inhibited sober self that never had the courage to speak out about his wife or his employer.

What are the familiar cases, and how do we decide them? How would we explain to ourselves why we just don't credit the person who refuses to get up in the morning? Why did nobody rescue Ahab, and why did I think that you would agree that anyone who loved Ahab, or even a conscientious stranger, should have held him down?

*   *   *

In some cases the person just doesn't seem to be all there. He is his usual self with something subtracted. The person who prefers not to get out of bed is thought to be not fully alert; his engine hasn't warmed up; he cannot remember or visualize the consequences of staying in bed or assess their importance. We may even believe that there are chemical inhibitors of brain activity that play a role in sleep, and until they have been washed or metabolized away his brain is not working. It is not a different *he*, just an incomplete one. The same may be thought of the person overtaken by fatigue or drowsiness, the person under sedation, and some of the people — the quieter ones — whose brains are awash with alcohol.

Then we have contrary cases, the people who are not only "all there" but too much. They are overstimulated or exhilarated. There are drugs that will do it, but so will success. So will relief — from anxiety or fear or suspense. In contrast to the drowsy, these people need restraint, not arousal. They can suffer a transient self-lessness and generosity, not withdrawal but hyperactivity. If the half-awake person can be described as somebody whose preference map is not fully illuminated, the overstimulated person is like one whose preference map, though illuminated everywhere, is too brightly lit in some places. The contrast has the same effect as partial darkness.

A third case is passion, or infatuation. We have the expression "marry in haste and repent at leisure," and some that convey the same thing more bluntly. But I include anger, patriotism, religious fervor, revenge, disgust, and all of those transient overwhelming moods that elevate certain values to absolute domination. Proposing marriage, joining the foreign legion, placing large wagers in support of one's opinion, abandoning one's family, and tearing up one's will are among the things that may be done in haste and repented at leisure.

Next is capture, or captivation. It is being glued to TV, absorbed in a novel, caught in a mathematical puzzle, engrossed in a symphony, or absorbed in frustration trying to fix a recalcitrant piece of equipment. This may be where to include fantasy; some of us are as readily captivated by daydreams as by that late movie or unfinished novel. A simple interruption will sometimes rescue the captive; other times he can still hear the siren song and may be as sneaky as an addict in getting back to that puzzle, story, or daydream.

My next set consists of phobias, panic, and extreme terror. The person who cannot dive off the high board or make the parachute jump, who cannot face an audience without an urge to flee, who suffers vertigo or claustrophobia, cannot make himself pick up a spider or put a kitten to death. I saw a movie in which a Scottish fisherman had his thumb caught in a giant clamshell. The tide was rising. With his knife he severed his thumb. I've wondered whether I'd have drowned before I could remove mine. The friendlier illustration is a child's loose tooth; tying the tooth by a string to a doorknob and slamming the door was the solution when I was a boy, and it illustrates how short the interval may be between the preference that the tooth be yanked and the succeeding preference that it not be.

Some of these are easy cases. But I mean easy to decide, not easy to cope with. If we've come across someone sitting in the winter woods freezing to death, drowsy and feeling no cold, and he refuses to jump to get warm, getting him to do it may be impossible; but deciding whether to obey his command to leave him alone should not be hard.

Some of these cases I no longer find easy. But there are at least some easy cases in every category I mentioned, and I tried to describe them with sufficiently prejudiced language to make you think of some easy cases. I have two more categories. The first is appetite. By that I mean food, drink, tobacco, and any substance that a person can eat or sniff or inject or rub on his skin that generates an addiction or habituation. (I could include here addictive activities, like gambling or golf or the morning newspaper; but they may be more at home in my earlier category of capture than here with nicotine and chocolate.) What keeps these appetites from being easy cases is that not everybody is more likeable sober than drunk. Some of the addictive narcotics may be harmful only because they are disapproved of and prohibited. And some attempts to quit cigarettes may be so doomed to failure, or to periodic relapse, that surrender is preferable to a fruitless pursuit of victory.

One more category is perseverance. Its obverse is procrastination, quitting. People who set themselves regimes of daily exercise, piano practice, or periodontal care often fall by the wayside. Joggers do not enjoy universal sympathy. Some good intentions abort for plain lack of serious dedication; and people who could bind themselves to a program might in the end find it a bore and regret it. I see all around me, and inside me, the occupational disease of procrastination. Many of us have to burden ourselves with deadlines or short-term goals to get anything written. Social controls play a role; the *Times Literary Supplement* for January 22, 1982, contained a splendid example, a review article by George Steiner on the life and work of the Hungarian radical Georg Lukacs. "When I first called on him, in the winter of 1957–8, in a house still pockmarked with shellbursts and grenade splinters, I stood speechless before the armada of his printed works, as it crowded the bookshelves. Lukacs seized on my puerile wonder and blazed out of his chair in a motion at once vulnerable and amused: 'You want to know how one gets work done? It's easy. House arrest, Steiner, house arrest!' "

* * *

Let me reexamine a few of these characterizations. The person who won't get up in the morning I said was not quite all there. Why does that count against him? Apparently because he cannot fully appreciate what it will be like to be late to work. But does the self who sets the alarm fully appreciate the discomfort of getting out of bed? My answer is yes. But notice: I am not in bed. I don't expect that to change your mind, but in more difficult cases I find it important to remind myself that when I think about these issues I am not impartial. I write only when I am awake, and the self that might prefer bed goes unrepresented.

In another respect we are not impartial. We have our own stakes in the way people behave. For my comfort and convenience I prefer that people act civilized, drive carefully and not lose their tempers when I am around or beat their wives and children. I like them to get their work done. Now that I don't smoke, I prefer people near me not to. As long as we have laws against drug abuse it would be easier all around if people didn't get hooked on something that makes them break the law. In the language of economics, these behaviors generate externalities and make us interested parties. Even if I believe that some poor inhibited creature's true self emerges only when he is drunk enough to admit that he despises his wife and children and gets satisfaction out of scaring them to death, I have my own reasons for cooperating with that repressed and inhibited self that petitions me to keep him sober if I can, to restrain him if he's drunk, or to keep his wife and children safely away from him.

And what about Ahab? When I first thought of mentioning him I thought him a dramatic illustration of an easy case. If I were Ahab, I thought, I would thank you afterwards for holding me down. But now I wonder what that proves.

If you hurt somebody so that I may live, my thanking you doesn't prove that you did right. If I say that in Ahab's condition I would like to be cauterized, you will notice that I say it with a fearlessness that makes my decision suspect. It is hard to find a way to call my bluff. I'm not about to be burned. If I were, I'd behave like Ahab, and you would not credit me with now having a full appreciation of where my interest lay.

Suppose I were to be burned and Ahab in the next room were to be burned also. Would you, while disregarding my personal plea, ask my advice concerning what to do about Ahab?

After you burn me and I recover and thank you, you give me the bad news: the other leg is infected and must be burned the same way to save my life, perhaps after a delay. Do I withdraw my thanks, in fear you'll think I want it done again? Does the delay matter?

How do we know whether an hour of extreme pain is more than life is worth? The conclusion that I reach tentatively is that we do not. At least, I do not. The question entails the kind of undecidability that many economists attribute to the interpersonal comparison of utilities. Most economists believe we have no way of testing, or even defining, what we mean by whether one person gets greater joy or utility or satisfaction out of a meal or a holiday or a warm room than another person, or out of spending some amount of money, and whether my enjoying something at your expense, my pleasure and your pain, can be added algebraically. That means that if you must cauterize Ahab's leg to keep me from dying there is no way to determine whether the little two-person society consisting of Ahab and me enjoys a net gain in utility when you spare him the pain and let me die.

The conclusion I come to is that I can no more decide this for myself, if it is I being burned and I dying, than I can decide for two other people.

Does it make it easier or harder if I imagine Ahab to be old, with only a few years of life to save at the cost of an hour's torture? You may well ask how, if I have just alleged that a judgment is impossible, it can then be easier or harder. What I have done is slip into the position that many economists take after acknowledging the impossibility in principle of that interpersonal comparison. It is to acknowledge that as a practical matter we do make decisions. We do not hesitate interminably over whether to favor some extra income for a poor person at the expense of a wealthy person, or whether to give our concert ticket to an enthusiast or to someone who merely likes music. Because we have to, we make such decisions.

So I must conclude that these decisions are not based on utility comparisons. What are they based on? In Ahab's case I think mine is taking sides. Which side am I on? Facing no pain I seem to be on the side of the Ahab that wants to live. I do not think I know how to make the effort really to decide whether his life is worth the pain. When I try, I find myself succumbing to the pain, and to keep my resolve for Ahab's sake I abandon the effort at comparison.

*   *   *

This ambivalence makes a difference in welfare economics, social choice, and political philosophy. In economics there is a well-explored field of individual rational choice. There has also been an interesting field of social choice, in which the singulary behavior of a rational individual is compared with a collective decision. We got used to the fact that in a collectivity there is no unanimous preference; we discovered that majority decision will not reliably point to a collective preference. And with continued work (of which Kenneth Arrow's is most widely cited) we have become convinced (some of us) that it is futile to model collective decision on the analogy of a single individual. I suggest that the ordinary human being is sometimes also not a *single* rational individual. Some of us, for some decisions, are more like a small collectivity than like the textbook consumer. Conflict occurs not only when two distinct human beings choose together but also within a single one; and individuals may not make decisions in accordance with the postulates of rationality, if by individuals we mean live people.

If we accept the idea of two selves of which usually only one is in charge at a time, or two value systems that are alternate rather than subject to simultaneous and integrated scrutiny, "rational decision" has to be replaced with something like collective choice. Two or more selves that alternately occupy the same individual, that have different goals and tastes, even if each self has some positive regard for the other (or one feels positively and the other does not reciprocate), have to be construed as engaged not in joint optimization but in a strategic game. There is no agreed weighting system for taking the alternate preferences simultaneously into account. And even the possibility of bargains and compromises is limited, if not precluded, by the absence of any internal mediator. It is hard for the different selves to negotiate if they cannot be simultaneously present. (Not impossible, perhaps, but hard.)[3]

So we should not expect a person's choices on those matters that give rise to alternating values to display the qualities typically imputed to rational decision, like transitivity, irrelevance of "ir-

---

[3] It is proposed by Jon Elster that typically one of the "selves" engages in forward planning and strategic behavior, making arrangements to constrain the other self's options, while the alternate self is preoccupied, when in command, only with the current episode. (He proposes that this asymmetry in strategic attitude is a basis for choosing the authentic self.) In the perhaps rarer cases of reciprocal strategic behavior, each party might engage an attorney to represent that self, empowering the attorneys to reach and enforce a mutually advantageous bargain. While this possibility has no legal standing, and, if it did, enforcement of the bargain might still not be manageable, it affords a conceptual possibility of negotiation between two selves that never simultaneously exist.

relevant" alternatives, and short-run stability over time. We should expect the kinds of parliamentary strategies that go with small-group voting behavior and the second-best choices that have to be made when rights and contracts are not enforceable. Depriving oneself of certain preferred opportunities — suppressing certain states that economists call "Pareto superior" — because the other self would abuse the opportunity becomes an expected tactic:

   — not keeping liquor (food, cigarettes) in the house
   — not keeping television in the house
   — not keeping sleeping pills in the house
   — not keeping a gun in the house
   — not keeping the car keys in the house
   — not keeping a telephone in the house
   — not keeping the children in the house

Dramatic cases of a *latent* rather than a *regular* alternate self are the anticipation of a self that will emerge under torture, truth serum, or extreme privation. Less dramatic are anticipated somnambulism and talking in one's sleep, scratching or removing dressings while asleep, and social affairs at which one is likely to lose his temper. Other familiar instances are choosing a restaurant where desserts or liquor are not served or luncheon partners who do not drink, doing embarrassing business by telephone to avoid loss of poise, and leaving money at home to avoid a shopping binge.

There is even a possibility that within a single human body a nervous system and brain and body chemistry can alternately produce different "individuals," no one of which is uniquely *the* person or self. In science fiction a human body can be an arena in which several extraterrestrials play out their careers. When several aliens come to inhabit an Earthling's body, one of them may sleep during daytime and another nighttime, one may have access only to certain memories or sensory systems, and they may compete to extend their spans of control over the Earthling body.

Is there anything like this among human beings? Maybe. Surgically, an individual is changed into "another individual" through frontal lobotomy. Lobotomy is irreversible as it has been practiced; but in principle one can imagine an irreversible removal (lobectomy) and a reversible lobotomy. With the latter, a person alternates between the self whose lobe is deactivated and the one whose lobe is functioning. The changes are described as dramatic enough to constitute a new personality. (The judicial system has had to decide, for purposes such as marriage annulment, whether it is the same person afterward.) Castration was an equivalently potent way of changing hormonally the value system of male human beings. It, too, is irreversible; but if we imagine castration accomplished chemically rather than surgically, it might be reversible.

Possibly the human being is not best modelled as a unique individual but as several alternates according to the contemporary body chemistry. Tuning in and tuning out perceptual and cognitive and affective characteristics is like choosing which "individual" will occupy this body and nervous system. When pressed I insist only that people can usefully, for some purposes, be viewed *as if* they were two or more alternative rival selves, but the more I reflect on it the more I wonder whether there is any reason for excluding the literal possibility.

*   *   *

The law does not like to distinguish these different selves, or to differentiate an authentic self from impostors. In America I cannot go to a fat farm, a non-smoking resort, or an exercise camp and legally bind the management to hold me when I ask to get out. The management cannot claim that it has contracted with the authentic "me" to make me stay even if my impostor self, the one that I went to the farm or camp to guard against, claims that "I" now want to get out. I can contract that they get no fee unless they succeed in keeping me; but the authentic "I" cannot sue them afterwards for improper release if they let me go when the wrong "I" insists on leaving. And they cannot protect their investment by impeding my departure when that other self gets control and says he is leaving and to get out of his way.

The law does not permit me to write a will that I cannot change, nor promise a gift and be held to my promise. If I think I am potentially dangerous, to myself or to others, the law does not permit me to commit myself voluntarily to the custody or guardianship of an institution that may hold me captive. I have to demonstrate that I am so dangerous, to myself or to somebody else, that I qualify for involuntary commitment. Dr. Jekyll can ask to be locked up for his own good, but when Mr. Hyde says "let me out" they have to let him out.

There are ways of getting around the law, but they do not involve straightforward recognition of a person's right to bind himself against himself. If I think it would be good for me to change my habits and location, to be kept away from people and places I know, to learn discipline, I can enlist in the Army. My enlistment is a contract in which the other party has an interest that can be legally protected against my defection. Legally the Army is not conspiring with my authentic self to frustrate the other self when it wants to go AWOL.

But if I cannot prevent my impostor self from asserting his (my) rights when it is his turn to be in charge, cannot lock him up against his will or make it a legal offense to sell him liquor, can I nevertheless deny him legally certain faculties that he might exploit when he is in charge? Can I claim that he was impetuous when he made that gift, and I'd like it returned; that he enlisted in a fit of patriotism after seeing an inspiring movie, or as a heroic gesture after being turned down by the woman he loved? Can I claim that he married under the influence of passion or liquor or a biorhythmical euphoria, and the marriage vow should be void? Can I arrange with my bank not to honor his check if he fails to pass a diagnostic test that determines whether he is the authentic

I or that impostor? The answer seems to be, not easily. Indeed, only very exceptionally. And usually only by claiming and demonstrating some recognized mode of mental incompetence. If I can be proved mentally impaired as I made a bequest the bequest can be invalidated and you have to give it back; but if I was simply out of my mind with joy, and suffering one of my occasional fits of impulsive generosity, I cannot claim that it wasn't "I" and that the gift wasn't "his" to give.

There are statutory ways of guarding against certain actions that might be taken by one's wayward self. But the ways that I know of merely constitute denial of legal sanction for actions that might be taken impetuously or under duress. The political process itself guards against impetuous decisions by requiring two readings of a bill, time intervals between announcement of intent and consummation of some activity, public notice, and other dilatory procedures. The chief mechanism seems to be mandatory delay, or the requirement that certain things, like marriage licenses, be issued only during daytime hours. Mainly they can guard against decisions taken by an impetuous self that gains control long enough to do the business but not long enough to outlast the delay.

The law can try to help one self guard against the other by protecting private efforts of "third" parties to cooperate with one of them. Surgeons may be privileged to tranquilize the patient who, if his head were clear, would in mid-surgery overrule the surgeon's decision. That, of course, is taking sides. The law may protect me in restraining you from some impetuous or violent act against yourself, an act that your other self would ultimately deplore. The law may protect me if I restrain you from rushing into the burning building to recover your negotiable securities, the family dog, or one of your children, especially if I unquestionably did it believing it to be for your own good, and more especially if it is judged indeed to have been to your benefit. But I probably cannot get away with kidnapping you to keep you from smoking or from getting tattooed, or to keep you a virgin, although your later recovery will probably protect me from your taking civil action. Recapturing you from a religious cult and washing out your brain is still in undecided legal status. The most serious cases are those that involve, one way or another, actively or passively, taking your own life — one of your selves taking the one life that you share.

Helping you die is not allowed. Attempts at suicide surely must often involve divided selves. The lesser acts that people seem incapable of making themselves perform, including those that involve a palpable phobia, suggest that taking one's own life except in the most painful or utterly hopeless situations or where it constitutes a desperate act of heroism, is bound to be internally controversial. Two selves alternate in hoping for death or life. The law takes sides. In effect and in explicit intent, the law sides with the self that will not die. Someone who lives in perpetual terror of his own suicidal tendencies can welcome the law's sanctions against people who might be importuned to help with the suicide. People for whom life has become unbearable but who cannot summon the resolve to end it have the law against them in their efforts to recruit accomplices. The self that wants to live, if there is one, has the law on its side.

*   *   *

There is a paradox. Full freedom entails the freedom to bind oneself, to incur obligation, to reduce one's range of choice. Specifically, this is freedom of contract; and it works through expectations. The behavior of others depends on what they expect of me; by restricting my own freedom of choice I gain influence over the choices of others. The results can be called "cooperation," "immunity," "bargaining power," or even "coercion." A textbook on the legal attributes of corporations emphasizes not only the right to sue but the right to be sued. The *promise* is an instrument of great power, but only if it is believed that one has to keep the promise (or make restitution).[4] The law recognizes this principle as long as the promise — the commitment, the obligation, the impairment of one's own freedom of choice — has a reciprocal quality and is *to* somebody else. The promise requires an addressee. One may not contract with himself.

This is a stunning principle of social organization and legal philosophy. One cannot make a legally binding promise to oneself. Or perhaps we should say that the second party can always release the first from a promise; and if I can promise myself never to smoke a cigarette I can legally release myself from that promise whenever I choose to smoke. It comes to the same thing.

Charles Fried provided me with the name for what has no standing at law — the *vow*. The vow has standing if directed to a deity and is enforced by whatever authority the deity exercises. And the vow as an expression of intent can receive social and institutional support if it is recognized by an established church. Religious and fraternal orders differ from the common law in providing moral support, even coercive support, for vows like abstinence, celibacy, penury, and dedication to prayer, good works, and even heroism. But the vow has no standing at law.

People nevertheless seek to make binding decisions through physical constraints and informal social arrangements. People ingest chemical antagonists against alcohol to induce nausea upon drinking. If people cannot lock the refrigerator they can wire their jaws shut. Devices can be implanted in people that will emit a signal to tell on them if they drink, or immobilize them if they

---

[4] "In order that I be as free as possible, that my will have the greatest possible range consistent with the similar will of others, it is necessary that there be a way in which I may commit myself. It is necessary that I be able to make non-optional a course of conduct that would otherwise be optional for me. By doing this I can facilitate the projects of others, because I can make it possible for those others to count on my future conduct, and thus those others can pursue more intricate, more far-reaching projects. If it is my purpose, my will that others be able to count on me in the pursuit of their endeavor, it is essential that I be able to deliver myself into their hands more firmly than where they simply predict my future course." Charles Fried, *Contract as Promise* (Cambridge: Harvard University Press, 1981), p. 13.

do. Castration and lobotomy have been mentioned as surgical techniques for permanently changing motives and incentives, and there are tranquilizers and negative aphrodisiacs to keep certain fears and passions in check. I have mentioned tying the tooth to the doorknob; one can ask a friend to pull the string instead. People avoid cues and precursors, the sights and smells that subvert their abstinent intentions; people dare not eat the first peanut, start an argument, begin the novel they can't afford to take the time to read, or turn on the TV because it is harder to turn off than merely not to turn on. The friend who will pull the string attached to the tooth, or extract a splinter, can also monitor calories and police cigarettes, or even push a person out of the airplane to help launch a skydiving hobby. But one can sometimes arrange a coercive environment, like offices in which smoking is not allowed or a job in an explosives factory, or make bets that are informally enforceable about weight control or cigarettes; and there are buddy systems, like Alcoholics Anonymous, whose moral support can be enlisted. We could invent some unconcealable testimony to one's dedication — dyed hair, or a tattooed forehead, imploring bartenders not to serve drinks and waiters not to serve desserts.

But nothing like contract law is available. I am not endorsing the idea that the law should be available to enforce unilateral vows. But there is little speculation about how the law might help and what the dangers and abuses might be.[5]

Actually, there is no a priori basis for confidence that enforceable contract is a generally good thing. People might just get themselves tied up with all kinds of regrettable contracts, and the custodians of legal wisdom might have decided that enforceable contract is a mischief. Suppose promises to second parties tended usually to get people into trouble, so that a wise legal tradition

---

[5] There is stimulating discussion throughout Jon Elster, *Ulysses and the Sirens* (New York: Cambridge University Press, 1979). I am indebted to his work and to his comments on this lecture. Most of the legal discussion I have found deals with mental illness and informed consent. See the reference to Rebecca Dresser's work in note 6.

would readily excuse people from promises incurred in haste, or in passion, or in disgust. Duress is recognized; if impetuosity were a problem, legally binding contracts might require something like a second or third reading before acquiring status. It is an empirical question whether the freedom to enter contract, the freedom to make enforceable promises, or the freedom to emancipate oneself from a nicotine habit would prove generally to be a good thing. But the social utility of recognizing the vow, the unilateral promise, through social or legal innovation is not much discussed. It may therefore be worthwhile to imagine what form such legal innovation might take.

A possibility is that the state become an enforcer of commitments that people would voluntarily incur and submit to authority. How would the state enforce my commitment to give up smoking, reading the comics at breakfast, or terrorizing my children? A possibility is that I grant the state a perpetual search warrant: the authorities may enter my home or search my person at any time without warning or court order, confiscating anything they find that is authorized in my original disposition to be confiscated. Another would be to allow denunciation: any observer, or anybody on a list that I authorize, could have me locked up or examined or searched, even punished — I having relinquished rights of cross-examination or immunity. House arrest might be voluntarily incurred; I can be locked up, kept in my home that has been purified of television, alcohol, tobacco, or inventories of food. I can be incarcerated and denied things I want or required to perform what I want to be required to perform — physical exercise, rapid reading, or writing this lecture. There could be a parole system: I oblige myself to report daily and be examined for weight, nicotine, heroin, or bloody cuticles. Curfews, and placing gambling casinos or bars off-limits to me, might be enforced by circulating my picture. I could be obliged to pay forfeit when caught in violation of my vow, giving up money or privileges or freedom; this would be like designing criminal law specifically for those who sign up to be subject to it. I could have license plates that do not permit me to drive at night, or that authorize any policeman to stop me and check for alcohol without regard to the First or Fifth Amendments. Or I might legally submit to a guardian; this would be like power of attorney, but would give somebody authority to have me subdued, to command that I not be served, to sequester me without my consent, or to control my bank account and my car keys.

The state might enforce contracts that I entered into for purposes of self-restraint. I make a bet that I will not smoke. A bet is equivalent to a penalty on my smoking. I can already make a somewhat enforceable bet if I bring a friend into it, but if he or she is a real friend, what I commit is respect rather than money, and if he or she is not a real friend and the amount of money is large, I probably do not have to pay because the bet is not enforceable. (Surrendering the money to a third party could help.) Still, the social coercion of bets among friends, especially small groups of more than two, in losing weight or giving up cigarettes is impressive. Insurance contracts might help: that medical insurance should be cheaper for people who do not smoke, because they make fewer claims on their medical insurance, is an idea that has some appeal even though it may not have much logic. (Smoking may kill people less expensively than most ways of dying.) But as an incentive people might be allowed to enter insurance contracts that imposed heavy penalties on proven relapses from declarations of abstinence, if there were unambiguous tests like body weight or cigarette stains that would permit a person to incur a high price for delinquency.

There has recently been some attention to the liability of bartenders for serving drinks to people who were already drunk and subsequently suffered accidents or violence. (There have been societies in which recognizable ethnic or racial types were ineligible for service of some kind.) We can imagine a category of voluntary outlaws, people who have irreversibly chosen never again to be served liquor, the law cooperating by making it a misdemeanor to serve such a person in a public place or even in private, there being some form of identification to establish liability. There might even be "citizen's arrest" of anyone caught smoking or drinking in public who had voluntarily enrolled among those for whom it is forbidden to smoke or drink.

An innovation might permit people to make contracts from the terms of which they could not release the second party. We contract that you may and must expel me from the airplane if I am unable to make myself jump, when I have signed up for parachute instruction. Or you may keep me in a cell until I sober up, lose weight, or go thirty days without smoking. When I scream to be released there must be some provision for inspection to see what it is that I am screaming about; but when it becomes clear that I am screaming only for cigarettes or heroin, or complaining that they don't feed me enough, the authorities will certify that the contract is merely being enforced and that my screams needn't be attended to any further.[6]

A difficulty with enforcing my vows is that there needs to be somebody with an interest in enforcing the rule on me. If you finance my business and I promise to return your investment, there is no need for the state to take any initiative; you take the initiative if I don't come through. But when I vow to do twenty pushups before breakfast, even if there are techniques by which to

[6] There is one proposal for a legally binding act of "self-paternalism" that has received attention, most recently in an exhaustive analysis by Rebecca S. Dresser, "Ulysses and the Psychiatrists: A Legal and Policy Analysis of the Voluntary Commitment Contract," *Harvard Civil Rights–Civil Liberties Law Review* 16 (1982), pp. 777–854. This is letting a patient give a psychiatrist authority to have the patient committed for treatment to an institution during an episode in which the psychiatrist prescribes such treatment and the patient refuses. In some ways this proposal is the epitome of our subject. It does, however, represent an extreme method, incarceration. All kinds of constitutional rights are impinged on, from the right to travel to the proscription of involuntary servitude. And it abuts the issue of involuntary commitment, which has a long civil-rights history. The careful analysis cited above demonstrates that concern for the merits of the case is only part of the matter; what might appear best for the rights and welfare of such patients could conflict with constitutional principles of much wider scope.

establish whether or not I comply, there is no one to bother unless we make it in somebody's interest to spy on me and denounce me to the authorities. We might offer rewards to people who catch me overweight and bring me in for weighing; that means assimilating the self-directed promise to criminal rather than civil law, which I think is a strike against it.

*   *   *

When I contemplate the aloofness of the law and the needs that so many of us have for help, including legal help, in binding ourselves for our own good (as we can bind ourselves in contractual exchange), I see a gap in our legal institutions. The law has grasped the paradox that freedom should include the freedom to enter into enforceable contracts; it seems to overlook the need that people often have, and perhaps the right that they should have, to constrain their own behavior for their own good. And this could mean, as I have mentioned, either submitting oneself to a personal "criminal law" with rewards for private enforcement, or entering into contracts entailing reciprocal obligations from which one could not release the second party. But having identified an important legal right that seems to be missing, I have to ask myself whether I really think it would be a wise society that permitted me to make irrevocable decisions, or decisions that I could revoke only at a high and deterrent cost. Do I really wish that there were some magical way that I could put certain acts forever beyond reach? Do I really wish that I could swear out a warrant for my own arrest in the event I violate some pledge, offering a large reward and complete immunity for anyone who apprehends me?

It is ultimately an empirical question whether even the right to enter a contract is a good one. If people were continually entering contracts shortsightedly we might want to protect them by requiring every contract to be ratified three times with prescribed time intervals between, to avoid contracts entered in haste. We have laws that deny minors the right to borrow money. We forbid indentured labor. People may not assign their earnings. Involuntary servitude may not constitutionally be voluntarily incurred. One cannot offer a pound of flesh as collateral, even if there is no other security to offer and one is desperate for a loan. But except for some constitutional and paternalistic safeguards, enforceable contract is popular because it has proved itself. Would the legal power of unilateral determinism, of eliminating options, of entering an enforceable vow, prove to be a blessing or a curse?

I do not know, but we can identify some dangers. One is that the wrong self gets the jump and legally protects its power to beat up the kids, keep liquor in the office, get fat or get skinny — I forget which is the "wrong one" here — or never to go jogging again. It is one thing to ask the law to recognize an individual's right to become legally forbidden or legally obligated to engage in certain acts or to live a certain way; it is something quite different for the law to select the authentic or legitimate or socially approved self and deny Mr. Hyde the right to oblige Dr. Jekyll to keep some of that stuff around that he drinks to become Mr. Hyde, or deny him the right to move away to where Mr. Hyde will have no place to play or people to play with when it is his turn to emerge.

Then there is changing your mind. I have arranged to pay a forfeit if I am observed smoking, and my informer draws a reward from that forfeit. I later discover that I am terminally ill and may as well smoke; or harmless tobacco is developed; or new research discovers that not everybody is susceptible to the hazards of tobacco, and specifically that I am not, and I'd like to enjoy smoking again. Can we design procedures for backing out of a commitment that was skillfully designed to make it impossible to back out?

Then there will be unforeseen emergencies in which people who were never to lay eyes on their children again need to see them, people who wanted their licenses revoked need to drive, or people who wanted to be confined need to be released. Procedures

that cannot be abused to undo the virtues of the original commitment would have to be devised.

I have heard expressions of concern that struggle builds character and the merchandising of "instant self-control" will weaken
the human spirit. I acknowledge the possibility but cannot help
comparing the argument to a similar argument we used to hear
against taking the pain out of childbirth.

We would want to avoid frivolous commitments — showing
off, momentary demonstrations, excursions into martyrdom while
under some kind of infatuation. (I conjecture that the tattoo has
been popular among youngsters precisely because it is indelible; it
is a permanent mutilation; it is an act of daring, precisely because
it admits no change of mind and shares if ever so slightly the
finality of suicide, loss of virginity, or enlistment in the foreign
legion.)

As both law and medicine deprecate suicide, they both deprecate castration of children. Sterilization is allowed for adults, but
I understand that psychiatrists are not at ease about sterilization
that may be undertaken for convenience by people who haven't the
maturity to appreciate how they may react at a later age. Children
under the age of contract can probably be dismissed from these
problems; but there is a slightly desperate quality to this whole
subject which suggests that this legal opportunity would be of
least interest to the people who could best claim sanity, adulthood,
maturity, responsibility, and emotional stability.

The objection that appeals to me most strongly is that people
may be coerced into "voluntary" self-denial, self-restriction, even
self-removal. A Los Angeles judge offered probation to a welfare
mother convicted of fraud on condition she let herself be sterilized,
thereby saving herself six months' incarceration; he was giving her
a free option only if — which was doubtful — six months was the
sentence he would have given her had her childbearing not been
at issue. Employers, parole boards, judges and probation officers,
even school admissions officers and spouses, not to mention various

moral minorities in the electorate, may demand assurances of both good behavior and good intentions as conditions for what they can offer, once those assurances are publicly available. Certain rights, like early retirement (even early death), can come to carry some implied obligation. (Imagine an option, perhaps upon application for marriage license, legally to forswear forever one's right to a divorce. Who could believe it was voluntary?) The "vow" itself, in its more traditional meaning as a profession of faith, was sometimes coerced by the vilest means. (Religious minorities have at least one advantage when the majority religion is one that a person must be born into — no coercive proselytising.)[7]

Coercion shows up in two ways, the one I just mentioned and the direct act of enforcement. If the government itself is responsible for enforcing the sanctions one has voluntarily incurred, in the manner of criminal law, there is both unpleasantness and an enlargement of that domain of government, the manipulation or harassment of individuals, that many of us like least. Enforcement by a private party, in the manner of civil law, would probably be felt to involve a noticeably lesser governmental role in the coercive enforcement. If damages only, not actual performance, could be claimed, the arrangements might be less effective but less threatening to society. Finally, there is the question whether the government should void or deny or prohibit privately available means of binding ourselves. Thomas Nagel has remarked that few governments any longer make it easy to enter into a permanently indissoluble marriage. Governments might regulate measures that

---

[7] Voluntary submission to polygraph testing is a perfect example. "In addition to its uses in prisons, the military, police work, FBI and CIA investigations, and pretrial examinations both for the prosecution and for the defense, the polygraph has also found its way into corporate America, where it is widely used for detecting white collar crime and for screening potential employees. This year, it is estimated, half a million to a million Americans, for one reason or another, will take a lie detector test." Alfred Meyer, "Do Lie Detectors Lie?" *Science 82* (June 1982), p. 24. Refusal to submit "voluntarily," like pleading the Fifth Amendment or declining to make financial disclosure, is construed as an admission of having something to hide.

operate directly on the brain. The implantation, requiring the services of a surgeon, of devices that monitor behavior could be discouraged by several means. I tend to feel that the dangers in allowing long-term renunciations of freedom are least when they do not depend on the government for enforcement; that leaves open whether government should deny the freedom to impair freedom where enforcement of contract by the government is not involved.

I do not conclude that the dangers are so overwhelming that we should continue to deny any legitimacy to the demand for legal status for these unilateral self-commitments. But I also do not conclude that we should discover a new disadvantaged minority, those that need help in self-defense against themselves, and acknowledge their right to enlist the law in their behalf. I conclude instead that there are probably innovations along the lines I have suggested, and that with care there might be some tentative exploration, with adequate safeguards and the expectation that it may be years or generations before we converge on a reasonable legal philosophy. The law is still groping for how to cope with rights to life and rights to death, rights of children and rights of the unborn, rights of separated parents, rights of the emotionally unstable or the mentally retarded, and the proper legal sanctions on drugs, adultery, contraceptive advice to minors, and the entrapment of drunken drivers. There should be no easy solution to this one.

I have spoken of the *legal* status of vows, but the issue could be more broadly formulated as one of social *policy*. The method could be legislative as well as judicial. Bartenders have been found liable for serving drinks to people who had already drunk too much and went on to get themselves destroyed by automobile. The liability could be established by legislation as well as by judicial interpretation. There have been and are societies in which particular kinds of individuals may not be served alcohol; what would be new is the provision for voluntarily putting oneself, perhaps with some indelible mark like a tattoo on one's forehead, in the statutorily recognized category of persons who may not be served.

*   *   *

The law aside, there are difficult discriminations in determining the authenticity of a request for help in somebody's dying.

If your moral convictions never permit you to help someone die, or even to let someone die in the belief that that is what he wants, no authentication is necessary, no request being admissible no matter how authentic. But if you wish to credit a request to be allowed to die, or a request to be helped to die, authenticating the source of the request — which self it is that is in command and controls the decision to make the request — is certainly important and probably difficult.

It is hard to imagine there being no question of authenticity. Death is so complete, so final, so irreversible, that a self that controls the decision may be unable to command the action. Inability to produce one's own death does not seem to be reliable evidence that one "really" prefers to live, any more than inability to cut one's own thumb out of its socket testifies to one's preferring to drown. Even asking for help may be subject to inhibition, and only a transient surge of determination could galvanize it. And while the self that is created by that transient surge may be the one that deserves recognition, it is not the only self involved.

We are dealing with an even more unambiguously "divided self" when the requests vacillate. To plead in the night for the termination of an unbearable existence and to express relief at midday that one's gloomy night broodings were not taken seriously, to explain away the nighttime self in hopes of discrediting it, and then to plead again for termination the next night creates an awesome dilemma.

How do we tell the authentic self? Maybe the nighttime self is in physical or mental agony and the daytime self has a short memory. Maybe the daytime self lives in terror of death and is condemned to perpetuate its terror by frantically staying alive, suppressing both memory and anticipation of the more tangible horrors of the night. Or perhaps the nighttime self is overreacting to nocturnal gloom and depressed metabolism, trapped in a nightmare that it does not realize ends at dawn.

The search for a test of the authentic self may define the problem wrong. Both selves can be authentic. Like Siamese twins that live or die together but do not share pain, one pleads for life and the other for death — contradictory but inseparable pleas. If one of the twins sleeps when the other is awake, they are like the two selves that alternate between night and day.

That both selves are authentic does not eliminate the issue. We must still decide which request to grant. But if both selves deserve recognition, the issue is *distributive*, not one of *identification*. We can do cost-benefit analysis and try to maximize their joint utility. But it is *we* and not *they* who are concerned with joint utility. The need for commensurable utility, for adding the desires of the one and the desires of the other, is like the need, under the authenticity formulation, for assessing the probabilities and the severities of the two errors: wrongly crediting the plea to die and wrongly crediting the plea to live. If the nighttime self is authentic we commit error in heeding the daytime self; but also vice versa. In the absence of certainty about which self is authentic, we have something like the distributive issue of dealing fairly with two selves that have opposite needs.[8]

---

[8] In discussion I find that responses to a hypothetical ambivalence about wanting to live and wanting to die are sensitive to the way the alternative preferences are described. If the choices are presented as symmetrical — a strong desire for life expressed at one time and a strong desire for death at another — people, while recognizing a grave conflict, elect to credit or defer to the voice in favor of life. But descriptions of actual patients who display the ambivalence often lend themselves to an alternative, nonsymmetrical formulation: there is a preference for *death*, and there is a horror of *dying*. Death is the permanent state; dying is the act, the transition — the awesome, terrifying, gruesome, and possibly painful event. Presented this way, the choice can be compared to Ahab's. Ahab can enjoy permanent relief — minus a leg, to be sure — only by undergoing a brief and horrifying event, as the

What about a promise made with certainty about the currently authentic self — authentic at the time the promise is made — to disregard the alternate self that may make an appearance? I ask you to promise to let me die, if necessary to help me, even to make me die, in certain gruesome and degrading circumstances that I specify in detail. Your promise is to disregard any countermand. No matter how much I plead to be left living you are to honor your obligation. And I urge you to contemplate, if tempted to heed the countermand, that it may be the voice of a terrified self that is incapable even of letting its terror be terminated.

The worst happens, and I plead persuasively. I claim that the self that demanded my execution couldn't know what I know now.

The same dilemmas can arise for pain rather than death. But the miraculous progress of anesthesia in our society makes Ahab's predicament uncommon, while the miraculous progress in medical life support is increasing the concern with dying.

If I can get relief from chronic pain only through an interval of acute pain and I cannot be sufficiently anesthetized to keep me from screaming for relief and pleading that the surgery be discontinued, there arises the ethical question. Do you let me change my mind when I discover how painful the ordeal really is that I committed myself to before I could ever know what it felt like to be in such pain? Or do you take note on my behalf that pain is short and life is long — or that pain will be past and life will be ahead — and not bother even to measure my pain's intensity?

Dying, killing, and suicide are unlike pain, confinement, disablement, and even torture, which, however horrendous, have a finiteness that death lacks in our culture. Imagine a patient allergic

---

permanent relief of death can be obtained only by undergoing a brief and horrifying event. Of course, the person whose momentary preferences are dominated by the terror of dying may not be able to cooperate in making this discrimination for us. Indeed he or she may misrepresent (even to himself or herself) the terms of the choice, just as people who face a frightening trip to doctor or dentist may misrepresent their symptoms. In somewhat the same way, the novice parachutist might be described as badly wanting *to have jumped* while frightened of *jumping*.

to anesthesia solemnly signing a request before witnesses that the operation about to be embarked on proceed irrespective of the patient's vehemently expressed later wishes that the pain and the operation stop. I expect the surgical team to abide by the request, secure in the belief that no punitive action could be taken against them until the operation had been completed and the pain had subsided, by which time the patient's original self, the one that signed the request, would again be gratefully in charge. I can even more easily imagine the surgeon's assuring the patient that the operation requires confining his head so that no request could be voiced, and confining his head, whether it were necessary for the surgery or not. (The rule might be: anesthetize the tongue if you cannot anesthetize where it hurts.)

Our thinking on this may be affected by the observation that, at our ages, examples of unbearable pain are usually episodes, like surgery or cauterization. When instead protracted intervals of pain are the lifetime price one pays for mobility or even for just living, doctors have to cope with patients who occasionally can't take it any more and who ask in desperation that the source of the pain, life itself, be removed.

We probably wouldn't hesitate to deny the request if it were a child. (It may be easier to cope with adults, especially elderly adults, the more childlike they become when at the mercy of a physician.) I don't know whether that is because we assume that the child's current self has a poor appreciation of the future, and other successive selves may be grateful that the younger self was not allowed to make that decision before they came on the scene. How many later selves have to endorse that early decision before we count a quorum and let those who have now spoken have their way at last?

Pain is often the obverse of dying. Dying is just the back side of the coin, when removing the source of the pain means removing life from the body. There is no later grateful self to express satisfaction if the doctor withholds relief, and no self able to thank him if he complies.

*   *   *

For centuries people were terrified by Hell, a condition worse than life itself, one that awaited after death, an inescapable sequel to which self-destruction made one especially susceptible. Death was no escape. But the audience for these remarks probably believes that death is the end of pain, an exit, not the entrance to an eternity of horror. And whatever the morality of suicide, it is probably not thought by many in my audience to be punishable by eternal damnation.

But the medical ability to keep people alive, to keep them alive irrespective of their wishes or despite them, and the legal obligation or ethical compulsion to do so — the obstinate unwillingness to recognize a right to death as well as a right to life — may have recreated Hell. While science and enlightenment were emancipating us from Hell after death, medical technology has recreated Hell as an end-stage disease. And our social institutions have made it a fate not easy to escape.

But expressing a wish to die or to live, when circumstances are tragic enough to make the choice genuine, is subject to multifarious dimensions of authenticity. The preferences themselves may not be voiced. Just as a person may be incapable of the initiative to commit so awesome an act, a person may be incapable of speaking about it. If the decision requires moral support or intellectual guidance, if one needs advice or at least an opportunity to discuss it, there is no way to discuss it without engaging another person; and the other person will be an interested party, perhaps himself unable to identify or to authenticate an expressed preference. Anyone intimate enough to be asked for help, even in arriving at a decision, is likely to have a selfish interest in the outcome, one that may conflict with his interest in identifying the authentic wish of the person whose death is at issue.

If I am the unhappy patient I may prefer to live but wish to die to stop being a burden to you. I may not want to burden you with guilt if I choose death, or to suggest that I think you resent my living. I may not be able to ask you to help me die to relieve you of the burden of me. And if I wrongly think you will benefit from my death, how can you persuade me my belief is wrong.

If you genuinely believe I prefer death, how can you be sure your own preferences are not mingled in your judgment of what is best for me, or of what I think is best for me? How can you avoid being suspected, even by legal authorities, of excessive zeal in helping me to relieve you of me? May the legal availability of a right to invite death acquire the character of an obligation? How can you keep your willingness to help me reach a decision to die from being, or appearing to be, an effort to persuade me? And how do several interested parties — kin and medical attendants — participate in the decision when they are themselves in dispute about the death and about responsibility for it?[9]

There is no graver issue for the coming century than how to recognize and authenticate the preferences of people for whom dying has become the issue that dominates their lives. This is the ultimate dilemma of authenticating the self, of discovering the legitimate sovereignty of the individual.

---

[9] I have written more on this in "Strategic Relationships in Dying," in Ernan McMullin, ed., *Death and Decision* (Boulder, Colo.: Westview Press, 1978).

INDEX

[201]